Brickhouse Mindset

Simplifying Self-Love & Manifesting Your Best Life

Che' Lovelight

Copyright © 2024 Che' Lovelight

All rights reserved. No part of this book or any portion thereof may be reproduced or used in any manner whatsoever without the express written permission of the author except as permitted by U.S. copyright law.

Printed in the United States of America

First Printing, 2025
ISBN 979-8-9923015-8-8

www.BrickhouseMindset.com

Dedicated to My BabyGirl.

You were Born a Brickhouse!
Thank You My Love, for allowing Mommy to share her gifts.
You have done this in immeasurable ways by teaching me so much about Love, self-care and the importance of being kind yet Fearless!
I wrote Brickhouse Mindset so that you will never have to ask who you are nor question your value.
Thank you for choosing me.
Mommy will always Love You More!

You Are My Greatest Inspiration!

Table of Contents

Preface

Part I: Developing The Brickhouse Mindset

- Chapter 1: **Introduction to Che'** 1
- Chapter 2: **What Is Your Why?** 9
- Chapter 3: **Welcome Brickhouse!** 17
- Chapter 4: **Laying Bricks** 26
- Chapter 5: **The Brickhouse Mindset Phase I** 39
- Chapter 6: **The Brickhouse Mindset Phase II** 79

PART II: Manifesting A Life That You Love

- Chapter 7: **Love Yourself** 95
- Chapter 8: **Optimizers for Manifesting Your Best Life** 109
- Chapter 9: **Overcoming Obstacles** 123
- Chapter 10: **Trust Your Intuition & Take Accountability** 131

PART III: Your Relationship with Yourself & Others

- Chapter 11: **Heal Baby!** 143
- Chapter 12: **The Brickhouse Body** 160
- Chapter 13: **Brickhouse Relationships** 177
- Chapter 14: **A Brickhouse Marriage** 259
- **My Closing Message** 276

Preface

From the moment we are born, society, our parents, and our environment mold us with their beliefs, expectations, and programming. However, many of us are never taught how to develop our own programming: a set of beliefs and thoughts that allow us to create the lives we want. We often measure ourselves against someone else's expectations, believe our desires are out of reach, and find ourselves trapped by self-imposed limitations and stress. But we indeed have the power to change how we see ourselves and our ability to shape our experiences.

This truth is most evident when we listen to people who have achieved their goals versus those who haven't. The successful ones speak of how they persevered and adjusted their thinking and strategies to overcome challenges. The unsuccessful ones often dwell on obstacles, missed opportunities, and their own sense of defeat. The difference between a winner and a defeatist often lies in how/if they believed in their goals and the choices they made along the way. No one is born a winner or a loser; it is the utilization or relinquishment of one's physical and mental power that makes the difference.

In many ways, our culture emphasizes discipline and achievement, often tying success to how well we conform to predefined expectations. Yet, it frequently neglects the importance of cultivating self-love and personal fulfillment as essential components of lasting success. These critical skills are rarely nurtured in our early years. Instead, we're encouraged to adhere to paths dictated by family, society, or cultural norms, with little regard for whether those paths align with who we authentically are. From a young age, we're encouraged to excel in school, sports, and various structured activities, all of which require discipline and measurable outcomes. While these activities shape our ability to work hard and persevere, they rarely foster the internal resilience or self-worth needed to navigate life's complexities.

This gap often becomes apparent later in life, when people face challenges that reveal their importance, and that discipline alone cannot solve. Without a strong mindset or self-love, achievements can feel hollow, relationships may lack authenticity, or true genuineness and setbacks can seem insurmountable. These moments of struggle reveal what we were never taught; that a resilient mindset and self-love are not luxuries, they are necessities. They are the tools that allow us to pursue goals that resonate with our true desires, not just those imposed upon us, and to find fulfillment in the journey as well as the destination.

A strong mindset involves more than simply pushing through challenges, it requires understanding how to adapt to setbacks, develop an optimistic perspective, and manage emotions in a way that serves our growth. Self-love is about more than just liking yourself; it's about valuing yourself deeply and treating yourself with the same care and compassion you would show to someone you cherish. It's about honoring your own needs, becoming clear on who we are beyond the expectations set by others, and making choices that align with your well-being and happiness.

Self-love and a strong mindset are deeply interconnected. Self-love gives you the confidence to pursue your dreams, while a strong mindset gives you the discipline and focus to achieve them. They work hand in hand to guide you toward living authentically, embracing your worth, and creating a life rooted in peace and purpose. Both are essential for manifesting the life of your desires and navigating challenges with grace and resilience.

For example, self-love might lead you to set a goal of improving your health because you value your body and want to take care of it. A strong mindset ensures that you stay consistent with your healthy habits, even when it feels challenging. Similarly, self-love might inspire you to leave a toxic relationship, while a strong mindset helps you navigate the emotional challenges of starting fresh. When these two forces work in harmony, you become unstoppable. You gain the clarity to define what you want in life, the courage to go after it, and the strength to overcome any obstacles along the way.

I've created the *Brickhouse Mindset* as an owner's manual to help women strengthen their minds and focus on their true needs and desires. A resilient mind is essential, not only in moments of stress and uncertainty but also as a foundation for lasting happiness, self-awareness, and fulfillment. It serves as a powerful tool for avoiding self-sabotage, making meaningful decisions, and living life to its fullest.

My focus is on women not just because I am one, but because as the creators and nurturers of life, when we align with our highest good, we have the potential to uplift and inspire everyone around us. By embracing our own growth, we set the stage for our partners, family, and friends to do the same, creating a ripple effect that elevates our collective well-being. However, the principles within *Brickhouse Mindset* are universal, benefiting anyone who seeks to build a stronger mindset and live in alignment with their purpose. I encourage you to share these lessons with your loved ones, including your partners and children, so they too can experience the power of a resilient, aligned life.

Brickhouse Mindset aims to demystify some of life's complexities and provide a framework for women to learn how to love themselves by first eliminating thoughts that do not serve them, focus on thoughts and actions that help them achieve their desired life and goals, and make decisions that lead them to a life that they love.

Every day, all day we make choices. Some may seem trivial, while others can be overwhelming. Yet, it's the accumulation of these decisions and our thoughts behind them that create the quality of our lives. If we were taught to master our mental power and the importance of making choices that support our mental wellbeing, we would make better ones. Choices don't just affect what we do but they also shape our self-identity and the state of our minds.

Unfortunately, many humans are comparing their lives to and/or imitating the lives that are presented for entertainment and programming, and it is destroying your psyche, peace, and potential. Depression, low self-esteem, competition, jealousy, toxic relationships, and self-sabotage are stealing valuable time from you creating the life you crave.

Life is Simple, but that doesn't mean Easy.

Brickhouse Mindset is designed to awaken you from life's distractions and provide a framework to help you push past the noise so that you can live the life of your desires. You owe it to yourself to live your best life, and you will never regret pursuing it. Creating a life that brings you peace is simpler than you may think, and the very fact that you've opened this book suggests that now is the perfect time to start.

Notice I said *simple*, not *easy*. Our emotions, desires, societal norms, and the intricacies of relationships and decision-making introduce layers that can make life feel anything but simple. Drama, heartache, betrayal, disappointment, stagnancy and depression are not easy either, but oftentimes, this is where we focus our attention to the detriment of our peace. Whether life is experienced as simple or complicated largely depends on how you approach and interpret your life experiences.

Will an abundant life manifest overnight? Most likely not, especially if you haven't yet been consciously cultivating the energy, thoughts, and actions that align with your highest potential. But once you do, you'll be tapping into the universal laws that are always at work, waiting to support your journey. When you begin to align your energy with your desires, you set in motion a powerful force that draws the right experiences, opportunities, and people into your life.

Remember, creating the life you want is a journey of consistent intention and growth. As you commit to strengthening your mindset and aligning with your purpose, you'll find that the universe responds in remarkable ways, opening doors and guiding you toward the abundance, peace, and fulfillment you seek. The more you cultivate this alignment, the closer you come to the life you've always envisioned, one step at a time.

Think of *Brickhouse Mindset* as your recipe for an abundant life. A quick, powerful guide to remind you how to love yourself, choose yourself and stay on the path towards your highest self. Towards peace, achievement, and happiness. Life is a journey meant to be enjoyed, and the quicker you get out of your own way, it will be.

My Dear Brickhouse!

Welcome to *Brickhouse Mindset*, your owner's manual for simplifying loving yourself and creating a life that you love by strengthening your mind, body, and soul.

– Love, Che' Lovelight (pronounced Shay)

Part I:
Developing The Brickhouse Mindset

- Chapter 1 -

- Chapter 1 -
Introduction to Che'

"Just because I make it look easy doesn't mean it is." Che' Lovelight

Ever since I was a young girl, I dreamed of writing a book that would make life just a little easier for people, especially for women. I saw it as a collection of life lessons that could help us all absorb and apply timeless wisdom to live our best lives. That seed has grown over time into what you now hold in your hands, *Brickhouse Mindset*, an owner's manual designed to empower you to embrace your inner strength, find clarity, and pursue your dream life with focus and intention.

As a child, I learned firsthand the impact of high expectations. Raised by very strict parents in a time when children were expected to be seen and not heard, I quickly learned the importance of obedience. Compliance wasn't optional, and stepping out of line came with severe consequences. My father was present but emotionally disconnected and mother held the reins firmly. She meant to protect me from life's hardships, but the unintended effect was that I grew up grappling with indecision, physical anxiety, and a tendency to overextend myself that continued through adulthood.

When it finally came time for me to take control of my own life, I was determined to do it my way, but I often felt overwhelmed. Even the simplest choices became a struggle because, for so long, decisions had been made for me, and I hadn't yet learned how to trust myself. In addition, I am an empath, someone who connects deeply with others by intuitively feeling and understanding their needs on a profound level. However, this gift often comes with a self-sabotaging tendency to prioritize the happiness of others above our own. The need to learn who I was and how to make decisions for myself led me to study the powers of the mind and spirituality shortly after college, ultimately laying the foundation for *Brickhouse Mindset* to be written decades later.

Despite my strict upbringing, I hold immense gratitude for both of my parents, and in relation to this book, my mother's guidance in particular. She taught me crucial lessons that many don't learn at home, and having battled my weight my entire life, she instilled in me a strong sense of self-esteem that saved me from being swallowed whole by the narcissistic lovers my empathetic soul attracted later in life. She often told me that I was beautiful, smart, and capable, but that you can't have everything, and my extra weight was my cross to bear.

This was one of the lessons I believe she got wrong, and through the lens of the *Brickhouse Mindset,* my perspective has evolved significantly. You absolutely can have what you want in life, regardless of the obstacles, as long as you align your mindset, energy, and actions with your desires. Limitations only exist when we believe in them, and when we're dedicated to doing the work, we open the doors to possibilities that once seemed out of reach. Your dreams are not defined by circumstances; they are fueled by your belief, focus, and determination.

Introduction to Che'

Growing up a chunky black girl in middle-class New Jersey with parents who divorced when I was 8 years old came with its own challenges, but this background has been a powerful force in my journey of self-discovery and self-actualization. My mother, a classically trained soprano and retired music teacher, made sure I was involved in music from a young age. She placed me in every choir she could find, nurturing my love for music and fashion. My father, a Jamaican immigrant and the first plant engineer hired by Bell Laboratories, now AT&T, shared his world of technology and love of the arts and gardening with me and my siblings. Together, they enrolled me in countless computer programming classes and engineering camps, igniting an early fascination with technology and innovation.

As I grew older, I knew I wanted to work within the music industry, but I wasn't sure exactly how. Although I loved singing, I didn't feel confident enough in my vocal abilities to pursue a career as a recording artist. Instead, I found myself drawn to the larger world of music and technology, and crafted a unique career that would combine my passions.

My journey eventually led me into the world of technology sales and corporate strategy, where I discovered that I could help shape industries, introduce groundbreaking tools, and empower others. Picture this, it's 2001, and I'm at the forefront of a technological revolution, introducing the Blackberry to corporate America, a device that would forever change how we connect. For the first time in history, email and the internet were right at our fingertips, reshaping communication and paving the way for the smartphones we rely on today. My technology sales career started right here in New York City and it was just the beginning.

I have had the privilege of introducing game-changing technology for some of the most respected corporations in the world, including AT&T, MCI/Worldcom and FranklinCovey, the creators of *The 7 Habits of Highly Effective People*. Through these roles, I have gained invaluable insights, honing my ability to communicate effectively and connect with diverse audiences. More importantly, I've developed a deep comprehension of how to simplify complex technologies and frameworks, making them accessible tools that drive efficiency and empower individuals to achieve their goals with clarity and precision.

I am incredibly proud of my career, which allowed me to experience profound self-actualization despite its ups and downs. My corporate career has been a whirlwind of exhilarating successes and unexpected challenges. I've weathered the highs and lows, one moment riding the wave of a major contract win, the next facing yet another layoff. In fact, I went through seven layoffs over the years, one of them while I was eight and a half months pregnant. These shake-ups came largely during the early days of my career, as the giant communications companies I worked for began gobbling each other up in a frenzy of mergers and acquisitions. They also allowed me time to expand my horizons and create my own stability.

My journey as a trailblazer wasn't confined to the corporate world; an entrepreneurial fire burned within me, pushing me to carve my own path in the music industry. I combined my skills in digital strategy, honed from also selling early web design and digital marketing services to Fortune 100 companies, and utilized it to

Introduction to Che'

create social media campaigns for artists and labels. My corporate background gave me an edge in understanding how to make digital opportunities mutually beneficial for all involved. If I saw an opening that aligned with my strengths, I found a way to make it happen.

Recognizing a gap in how R&B music was represented online, I decided to take matters into my own hands. In 2005, I launched one of the very first websites dedicated to promoting both independent and major R&B artists on the internet. It was my dream company, a platform I built from scratch including booking, recording, editing and writing nearly every article and video interview.

My connections in the corporate world served me well in this new venture. By that time, I had built relationships with key players at Sony Music, Jive Records and Universal Records through my sales of BlackBerrys and two-way pagers. These relationships allowed me personal access to some of the most powerful people in music and opened doors for me to interview a wide range of iconic R&B artists, from the legendary Teena Marie, Patrice Rushen and Regina Belle to Charlie Wilson, Tank, Raheem DeVaughn, and Syleena Johnson who are still thriving today.

From there, I expanded into artist management and music tour & festival production, immersing myself even deeper in an industry undergoing rapid growth and change. It was the time when "the blogs" wielded tremendous influence, capable of making or breaking artists online overnight. I understood that my background in digital strategy and my network could be powerful assets in helping artists navigate this evolving landscape. Every step forward was built on the relationships and skills I'd cultivated, bridging the worlds of technology, media, and music; proving that with passion, adaptability, and vision, there are always new paths to be forged.

This journey led me to an incredible opportunity: working under the mentorship of Dame Dash, a pioneer and legend in the industry. I had the privilege of working within the infamous DD172 media collective he built in SoHo, a creative haven that could have been modeled after Andy Warhol's Factory. Dame was the OG godfather of the scene, mentoring a diverse mix of A-list and independent artists, rappers, and producers within the walls of an old car dealership converted into a vibrant cultural hub. Here, art and music collided in real time. Artists collaborated, writing lyrics in cyphers, then capturing the essence of the city in raw, captivating videos that incorporated the dopest music and visuals of the moment.

Working within this powerhouse collective was inspiring. It taught me the importance of authenticity and the power of storytelling through music and visuals, reaffirming my belief that the most meaningful success comes from pushing boundaries and embracing your unique creative voice, with or without a budget. This experience wasn't just a career milestone; it was a testament to what can happen when we bring our full selves to the work we love, daring to create spaces where innovation can flourish.

I share these experiences because I recognize that, in our culture and celebrity often equates to success, respect, and believability, and I need as many bricks as possible to make my testimony and this book appealing to the masses.

But beyond that, I want to show what's possible when you believe in yourself and capitalize on the opportunities around you. I didn't have a roadmap for my career. There was no blueprint guiding

Introduction to Che'

me toward a path that blended technology, music, and media; I just dreamed, found work I was passionate about, and kept pushing forward. This journey has taught me that fulfillment doesn't have to be a distant goal or a luxury reserved for a select few.

You don't need to grind away at something that drains you to find success.

I built a career around the things I enjoyed, connecting people, building relationships, and creating something meaningful. My hope is that *Brickhouse Mindset* inspires you to do the same: to embrace your unique path, trust your strengths, and pursue a life that feels true to you, no matter how unconventional it may seem.

My Why

What's the secret sauce behind the career and life I've built? Beyond my professional experience, it's my unwavering belief in the power of personal empowerment and happiness. For over 20 years, I've delved deeply into the realms of spirituality, mindset mastery, and the wisdom of some of the world's most profound philosophers. These studies have shown me how to harness the incredible power of the mind to discover joy, chase dreams, and turn meaningful goals into reality.

I've also come to understand the critical role of personal responsibility in using the Universe's omnipotent powers to fulfill our life purpose. This realization inspired me to create *Brickhouse*

Mindset, a framework designed to help women cultivate self-love, resilience, and intentionality. It's a simplified approach to manifesting the life you desire, by focusing on your goals, loving yourself, and making choices that bring you closer to the life you envision.

You'll read more about my journey in this book and those to come, but I want you to know that I too have struggled to stay focused on the positives. I've endured the sometimes traumatic roller coaster of life by living through magical highs, and excruciating lows. I've created careers that filled my spirit and my bank account, yet I've also encountered near soul-crushing experiences with narcissists and career instability. My life has been far from perfect, yet it's one I'm grateful for, full of lessons that I believe are worth sharing. Lessons I hope will serve as a source of inspiration and a roadmap for others on their own journeys.

By now I have mentioned the topic of the narcissist a few times, but this book is not about narcissism. It is written by a survivor of narcissistic abuse who maintained her own light and wants every woman to cultivate her strength by focusing on first loving herself, so that she does not succumb to darkness and insecurity.

If I can help even one woman become her best self, which inspires her partner, friends, and family to do the same, I will have fulfilled my purpose. The ripple effect of one woman's healing can touch countless lives, ultimately influencing generations. Through *Brickhouse Mindset*, I aim to ignite that ripple, healing myself and anyone ready to embrace a life of purpose, love, and peace.

- Chapter 2 -

What Is Your Why?

Brickhouse Mindset Shift: I owe it to myself to live my Best Life!

Ok Brickhouse, now that I have shared a little about me, I want you to know that understanding who you are and what you really want out of life is the first step in this extraordinary journey towards becoming a Brickhouse, towards loving yourself and living your best life.

This is your "why", and to best wield this powerful instigator for change, it is essential for you to show love for yourself each day so that you can grasp the depth of your identity and value. This will best set you up to successfully live your best life and achieve your dreams. When you begin to identify the aspects of yourself that you love and admire, something magical happens, you start treating yourself with the respect and kindness that you fully deserve. You develop an appreciation for your unique qualities, talents, and attributes, and expect others to treat you accordingly.

Next, it is essential to grasp that you are a divine gift, and that every individual has a unique purpose. Despite what you may think, your purpose doesn't have to involve fame, wealth, or grand accomplishments. Most of us aren't here to become millionaires, influencers, or Olympic athletes. Instead, your purpose can be one action or a series of actions, creations or experiences.

Regardless of if you believe you know your purpose or not, your presence in this world is significant, and your impact is real. A great example of this is when you smile at someone or say something inspiring to them, this simple act can change the trajectory of their entire life. That one moment can not only change one person's life but can also change the world. That one moment can be a part of your purpose and you may not have even known it. Your purpose doesn't require a monumental contribution to society; it can simply be to be yourself.

Your life is a gift and living it to its fullest potential is a gift to yourself. When you understand this and approach life by loving who you are and nurturing your well-being, you naturally attract a life that fulfills you; and that, at its core, is the purpose we all share.

Why? Because God is love, so that means that you are love, and loving yourself is the foundation of leading a meaningful life. It sets the tone for every aspect of your existence, influencing how you interact with others, how you approach challenges, and how you navigate your journey. Self-love is not selfish, nor is it merely a buzzword; it's a crucial element that shapes your self-worth and self-acceptance. When you love yourself, you respect your inherent value and embrace your unique qualities. This acceptance fosters resilience, empowering you to face life's ups and downs with confidence and grace.

Self-love cultivates a positive mindset, allowing you to appreciate your strengths and acknowledge your weaknesses without harsh judgment. It encourages you to prioritize your well-being and make choices that align with your true desires. When you love yourself, you become your own biggest supporter, celebrating your accomplishments, no matter how small, and treating yourself with the kindness you would extend to a dear friend.

Why should you love yourself? Because you exist. When you ask a parent why they love their child, it is because they exist, and there is usually no need for explanation beyond that. A parent loves their child not for their achievements, appearance, or behaviors, but simply because they are their child. They show their love in different ways, but the requirement for love and self-love is simply because you exist.

Loving yourself is not just a nice idea or a feel-good mantra, it's the most important responsibility you have in life.

Self-love is the foundation upon which everything else you want in your life is built: your relationships, your dreams, your resilience, and your happiness. Without it, you'll find yourself constantly seeking validation from others, doubting your worth, and allowing circumstances to dictate your sense of fulfillment. But when you embrace self-love, you unlock your power and give yourself the permission to live authentically, unapologetically, and joyfully.

Unfortunately, we live in a society that breaks down our sense of self love in many ways, including cultural standards, beauty norms, materialism and an over emphasis on a supposed normalcy rather than individuality, but once you accept the fact, that none of that actually matters, and that the most important thing you can do for yourself is to love yourself, your life will change in profound ways.

In this journey toward your best self, begin by simply deciding to take the best care of yourself and to appreciate yourself. Take care of your mind, body, and soul, and in doing so, uncover the unique strengths and beauty that make you who you are. This is where the journey begins: with self-love, self-discovery, and the commitment to nurture the greatness within you.

As we begin to embrace who we are and design a path to becoming our best selves, I want you to think about who you are and what you love. What are you good at? What brings you joy? How do you want to feel every day, and who and/or what type of people are a part of this beautiful existence? What do you want to achieve in life and why are you embarking on this path towards fulfillment? Is it the desire for peace, a healthier lifestyle, the dream of writing a book, launching a business or invention, the pursuit of love, financial comfort, or something else entirely? Your "why" is your compass, guiding your actions and keeping you motivated.

Once we've identified who we are and what we want, the next crucial step is addressing the obstacles that often stand in our way. Many times, when it comes to living our best lives or achieving our ideal health, we sabotage ourselves. We allow excuses, doubts, and procrastination to hinder our progress.

Let's consider this: most of us need to work to support ourselves, and these responsibilities naturally become priorities because we know that without them, our lifestyle would be compromised. Even if you're fortunate enough to have your needs supported by others,

What Is Your Why?

there are still essential things you must do to stay healthy, grounded, and functional in society.

Similarly, when you're striving to live your best life, certain actions and decisions must take priority. Just as paying bills or putting food on the table is necessary to sustain your lifestyle, you must also focus on the steps needed to nurture your best self and create the life you desire. Prioritizing your personal growth and well-being is as crucial as any other responsibility in your life. It's the foundation upon which everything else is built.

My Dear Brickhouse, please leave no room for excuses, self-doubt, or procrastination when it comes to achieving your best you. When we sacrifice our goals, this can ultimately result in a dissatisfied life and even depression. A Brickhouse does not entertain defeat because she knows that flexibility, rest, and continuous learning are all necessary to achieve her desired lifestyle, so there is no defeat. This level of internalization is what sets you on the path to living your best life and how quickly or smoothly you get there.

I must stress here that it is not important that you put restrictive timelines on success, but that you work towards it. I will teach you how to create a lifestyle that supports the achievement of your goals and makes things easier. There is no need to add stress to your life, the goal is to alleviate stress so that your life is filled with experiences and feelings that make you feel good, and that lead you towards the beautiful life of your dreams. Sure, work does not always feel good, and procrastination works against you, but I want you to fill your journey with experiences that do make you feel good, encourage you, and make you feel more and more optimistic about achieving your goals so that the work becomes more and more rewarding.

So Brickhouse, let's embark on this journey together, knowing that self-discovery, self-appreciation, and unwavering commitment to your goals are the keys to unlocking your potential and creating a life that resonates with your truest self. It won't be easy, but the rewards are immeasurable, and the journey itself is a testament to your resilience and excellence.

Homework

Take a deep breath, then set aside some time to reflect on who you are in this moment. Think about what's happening in your life; what's working, what isn't, and where you desire to be. Use the following journal prompts to document and evaluate both the life you see now and the life you envision. Begin with the first three prompts, then choose at least three additional prompts from each section. Write your answers thoughtfully to gain a clearer understanding of who you are, what you desire, and what may be holding you back.

Journal Prompts

- 50 things I am good at. (Yes, 50!)
- 50 things I love about myself.
- Ask 5 people from different aspects of your life (friends, family, coworkers, strangers) what they love about you.
- What are my passions and interests?
- What activities make me feel most alive and fulfilled?

What Is Your Why?

- What do I envision my ideal life to look like?
- What do I enjoy doing that makes me lose track of time?
- If I could _____ for the rest of my life and not worry about paying my bills, what would that be and why?
- What are my Top 10 Bucket List items?
- What do I want to accomplish in the next year? Five years? Ten years?
- What are 5 of my most memorable experiences and how did they make me feel?

Now here come the hard questions.

- What are my biggest fears or doubts holding me back from pursuing my dreams?
- What do I not like about myself and where does this belief come from?
- Who first told me that I was not good enough and why?
- What excuses or justifications do I make for not taking action towards my dreams?
- How have I prioritized other people's expectations or obligations over my own dreams?
- When was the last time I took a risk and what was the outcome? What did I learn about myself?
- What do I continuously put off for later and/or avoid?
- If I were to leave this earth tomorrow, what would I regret not pursuing?

The first set of questions is designed to help you explore who you are, what you want from life, why you're working to become your best self, and how you envision your ideal life and purpose on this earth.

The second set delves deeper, uncovering ways in which you may be holding yourself back from reaching your potential. This is known as Shadow Work; identifying and working through the beliefs and patterns that keep you stuck in self-doubt, fear, or self-criticism. Through this process, you'll begin to dismantle these limiting beliefs, freeing yourself to embrace a new identity that aligns with self-love, confidence, and purpose.

– Chapter 3 –
Welcome Brickhouse!

Brickhouse Mindset Shift: Becoming a woman of strong mind, body and soul requires small everyday decisions that demonstrate my love of self.

My Dear Brickhouse, I believe with all my heart that we owe it to ourselves to love ourselves and live our best lives! To not only feel good about who we are, create enriching experiences, and achieve our dreams, but also to share our best selves with the world. In doing so, we inspire others to also work on becoming their best selves, creating a ripple effect that resonates through generations, ultimately building a better world.

The *Brickhouse Mindset* is designed to guide you in aligning your thoughts and actions, with the woman you aspire to be. It's about living the life you yearn for and attracting the people, experiences, and opportunities that resonate with your true self, while navigating life with resilience and optimism. In essence, The *Brickhouse Mindset* serves as an owner's manual for loving yourself and manifesting a life that you love. One that brings you joy, purpose, and lasting fulfillment.

This isn't just a book of theory. It's a framework for empowerment, a system for healing, and a reminder that you are the co-creator of your own life. You will first learn how to gain control over your mind and the beliefs that keep you from loving yourself and maintaining peace within. You will then learn how to focus your thoughts and actions on the desires of your heart, while creating a lifestyle that best supports your efforts. My goal is to simplify self-love and ways to honor and achieve your highest good, with the support of the universal and spiritual laws that have governed humanity for eons but have been masked by society and religion so that the laywoman will not have the guidance that was divinely gifted to her and her ancestors.

Manifestation is a journey, and this book is your map. It's about teaching you how to elevate your energy, align with your desires, and live intentionally every single day.

Through self-love, accountability, and practical steps, you'll learn how to co-create a life that feels as good as it looks. This is your invitation to become a Brickhouse: resilient, self-aware, and unshakably aligned with the best that life has to offer. You deserve everything good that this world has for you. Let this owner's manual show you how to claim it.

As women, we sometimes enter relationships or carry heavy responsibilities that lead us to lose sight of who we are. I never fully comprehended how this could happen until it happened to me. When we prioritize others' needs and expectations at the expense of our own, we can lose our sense of self, our personal growth and often, our self-love.

Welcome Brickhouse!

After giving birth to my daughter who taught me what true love is while I was enduring a marriage that made me indifferent and accepting less than the minimum from myself and others, I looked up one day and asked, "who the hell is this woman?" I had accomplished so much, but I was no longer my happy, vibrant self. My body was in its worst shape, and I wanted nothing more than to get back to my inner Diva. I felt like a stranger both mentally and physically and realized I had handed the keys to my life over to someone else, and that this life was no longer comfortable for me.

My marriage was unbalanced and unfair. I was working hard to achieve someone else's dreams while carrying the weight of most of the responsibilities and was not at all appreciated for it. I was living a life full of unnecessary obstacles. I allowed myself to be a passenger in my own car and none of this was OK!

Once I woke up and realized how much of my power I had relinquished, I was determined to regain my strength and sense of self. I had allowed someone else's voice to overpower mine and I knew better. Having read numerous books, and learning from spiritual gurus, physicists, and who we now call life coaches, I had already learned the power of the mind, the universal all, and how to use it to create many miracles in my life; but I realized that I was no longer doing the work on myself. I even found an old journal where I was trying to manifest for my ex-husband, and I had to laugh at myself because it doesn't work like that, especially if that person is working against you and themselves. Once I refocused on improving every facet of my life, everything changed.

Now, my mission is clear, to assist millions of women in learning how to love themselves by finding inner peace and becoming

Brickhouses, women of strong minds, bodies, and souls. But let's pause for a moment and ponder the term "strong woman' or more specifically since I am one, "strong black woman". It's a phrase that has been with us since my youth, but what does it really mean? In many ways, this label has inadvertently caused harm, implying that we must endure pain and hardship to embody the essence of a strong woman. This misconception is deeply damaging. If most of us believe in God or some higher power that is likened to a parent or a leader, would they want us to suffer? Do you want your children to suffer? I hope not.

Strength isn't about inviting unnecessary suffering into our lives like I did.

Strength is cultivated through a process that equips us to withstand challenges and adversity, reinforcing the mental and emotional muscles required for growth. It's about utilizing lessons to overcome some obstacles while wisely avoiding others.

The *Brickhouse Mindset* will help you cultivate that strength by focusing on the importance of self-love, so that you can create a life that you love. This framework will help you feel better in the next moment and align your thoughts and actions with your highest good. This, my friend is the foundation of inner peace, and a life well lived. After all, how can you define love, peace and happiness without feeling good? How can you achieve without aligning your thoughts and actions with success?

Welcome Brickhouse!

Definition of a Brickhouse

In this journey towards your best self, it is crucial to have a clear definition of what it means to be a Brickhouse and why this aspiration is worth pursuing, so, let's start our adventure by defining the essence of a

Brickhouse: i.e. a Goddess, Divine Feminine, Empress, or Queen.

At its core, the term "Brickhouse" encapsulates self-love, wisdom, beauty, and solidity. Think of a well-built structure that stands tall, unyielding to the elements. When we refer to a Brickhouse of a woman, we envision someone who embodies these qualities. She is not only beautiful, but her allure and confidence radiate from within, leaving an indelible mark on everyone she encounters. It is a presence and energy that is not only seen but felt by anyone she meets. A Brickhouse is a woman who is self-assured, who knows her worth and what she deserves, which is the best from herself and those around her.

A Brickhouse is also a woman who makes sound decisions that set the stage for exceptional experiences, enriching relationships, and a life overflowing with abundance. She invests in herself by nourishing her body, heart, and mind with wisdom, enabling her to confront life with a profound advantage, a reservoir of knowledge and inner strength. This strength can be acquired through life's trials and tribulations or by attentively absorbing and applying the valuable lessons bestowed upon her. My mission is to equip generations of Brickhouses with the latter, so they can bypass the time-consuming mistakes of life and revel in its beauty, joy, and triumphs!

One prominent example of a Brickhouse is Serena Williams. Her name resonates with power and overstepping obstacles, and when you think about her, you can't help but admire her achievements. She exudes goddess energy through her unparalleled confidence, resilience, and grace, both on and off the court. She radiates strength and self-belief, breaking barriers while inspiring others to embrace their power, proving that true greatness is born from self-love, discipline, and authenticity. Serena Williams is the epitome of a Brickhouse. But was she born this way, or was she meticulously molded, trained, and stretched to become the greatness we see today?

Consider the countless hours she has dedicated to strengthening her body in the gym, the relentless practice on tennis courts to refine her craft, and the pursuit of knowledge through obtaining both an associate and a bachelor's degree to support her ventures in business and philanthropy. Her parents also worked diligently to develop the confidence necessary for her and her sister Venus to often be the only black children on the courts, to practice instead of play, and to stay away from the distractions of inner-city life. She didn't cut corners or take shortcuts. Serena was carefully prepared to face every challenge, both mentally and physically. She exemplifies the essence of a Brickhouse.

Now, your personal goal may not be to achieve Serena Williams' level of physical dexterity, launch businesses, or become an international icon; however, why not aim to become your best self

Welcome Brickhouse!

so that you can find happiness and peace rather than be weighed down by life's disappointments and challenges? Becoming your best self necessitates a constant stream of daily decisions that propel you toward peace in your mind, love in your heart, and accomplishing your goals. You accomplish this by consistently choosing what you want and what is best for you. The more you do this, the easier it will be to continue to do so. If you don't know what you want, go back to the homework in Chapter 2 and identify how you want to feel about those things, accomplishments, people, and experiences that you desire. The feeling is the goal.

In essence, life is a series of choices, and the quality of our life can largely be attributed to the quality of our choices. The more choices we make for our betterment, the better our lives. The more choices that we make that do not work towards our best, the more challenging life can be. In addition, any choice can be easy or hard depending on our mindset or how we think about the choice or its options, but the more we make choices that are for our benefit, the easier it will become to continue to do so.

This book is designed to simplify how to first master our minds and make better choices in efforts to love ourselves and the lives that we create. Sometimes, we unknowingly complicate matters by failing to choose what is best for us or doing things out of panic instead of working within the flow of life. Once you fully grasp your power, your best life will unfold before you, and you will find yourself creating the life you've always desired with more ease.

I repeat, life is not always easy. It is undoubtably filled with challenges, heartache, pain and disappointment, but it is also filled with joy, fun, leisure, ease and abundance. Embracing the

Brickhouse Mindset means acknowledging that life's journey is complex and woven with both struggles and triumphs. Your quality of life will improve when you choose to appreciate the good moments while learning from the hard ones. Each challenge presents a chance to adapt and become a stronger version of yourself.

My aim is to guide you to focus on the peace that exists within each moment, rather than the struggles we often find ourselves holding onto. By shifting your perspective, you can transform your life experience from one that feels like a constant battle into something closer to a beautiful, fulfilling journey. It's about creating balance, acknowledging life's challenges while fully embracing and celebrating its joys.

Through this mindset, you can cultivate resilience and a deeper appreciation for the journey ahead, allowing you to navigate life's ups and downs with grace and confidence. Together, let's work toward making your reality more fulfilling, empowering you to create a life that actually reflects your desires and aspirations.

One of the most powerful things you can decide for yourself would be to choose to release worry and instead choose thoughts that resonate with your desires and make you feel good. By intentionally choosing to find peace and happiness in each day, you will begin crafting a lifestyle that will support your journey toward your best self. You will incorporate self-care, maintain positive mental and physical health practices, and develop tools to implement in the face of stress and adversity. These choices encourage you to continue making sound decisions. You are working with the flow of your good which does not equal perfection

Welcome Brickhouse!

but should lead you to peace. This is how you choose yourself. This is the essence of the *Brickhouse Mindset*.

You are not a mere spectator in your life, passively accepting what is handed to you or following paths predetermined by others. You possess the power to shape your life the way you desire it to be.

- Chapter 4 -

Laying Bricks

Brickhouse Mindset Shift: I have access to all that there is to manifest my dream life.

Now, let's break down some universal laws, definitions and concepts that will aid you in knowing that you have infinite power to create the life of your desires by changing how you view yourself and the world.

The 12 Universal Laws can help you as a Brickhouse, navigate your life with intention and purpose. These laws are not just abstract concepts; they are fundamental principles that govern the universe and our experiences within it. They encompass concepts such as the *Law of Attraction*, which emphasizes the power of your thoughts and intentions to attract the same to you, and the *Law of Cause and Effect*, which illustrates how your actions directly influence your outcomes.

The *Law of Vibration* states that everything in the universe is energy vibrating at different frequencies. In simple terms, frequency is the wavelength, vibration, or "vibe" of something. When you focus your mind and energy on the same frequency as the belief, goal, or desire you're aiming for, you align yourself with it, attracting it into your life.

This is how these universal laws overlap and work together, providing a foundation for manifestation, how we actively create our experiences, dreams, and desires. But it's also how we inadvertently create lives that leave us feeling stuck, unhappy, or even depressed. If you believe that "this is as good as it gets" or that "life is hard," you'll continue to operate within that frequency, attracting more of the same. It is only by shifting your mindset, focusing on higher vibrations, and aligning with what you desire, that you can start to bring positive change into your life.

These laws will be in play whether you believe in them or not, so by familiarizing yourself with them, you can harness their power to create the life you desire, cultivate deeper self-love, and foster fulfilling relationships. I am sure that you have heard of many of these laws, but their effectiveness lies in your willingness to reflect, adapt, and take inspired action to utilize them to your benefit. By incorporating these laws into your mindset, you will know that the entire universe is working with you so that you will achieve the lifestyle that you believe in.

The next key concept to grasp is that we are all connected, in ways deeper than we realize. Our minds are also connected to a greater consciousness, the One Mind or Creative Source, which created the universe, its laws, and everything within it. This is the essence of the *Law of Divine Oneness*, which emphasizes the interconnectedness of all things. Oxford defines the mind as "the element of a person that enables them to be aware of the world and their experiences, to think, and to feel; the faculty of consciousness and thought." Your mind, as part of this divine oneness, is a spark in the process of creation itself. Before anything can be created, it must first be thought of, right?

When we think of The Most High God, the Divine, or Spirit, titles I use interchangeably, we're referring to the ultimate creator of all that exists. Spirit is in each of us and in everything around us. It is funny how people get so scared to say that they are a god while at the same time believing that they are a child of God and that god lives within us. God is The Most High God, but that god energy runs through each of us, and you need to tap in to this creative energy. Everything that has been created came from an act of Spirit, and/or through an actual birth. When you tap into a thought or frequency, you're connecting with this oneness, the universal source that encompasses all possibilities. With sustained focus and intention, you align with the laws of this infinite field of potential, allowing everything you need to come together to bring your desires into reality.

Think of this interconnectedness like the internet or even ChatGPT. When you seek information, you type in a question, and almost instantly, answers appear, whether from a website, book, image, or song. Every bit of that information, every thought, desire, or impulse, exists within The All. This All encompasses everything, thoughts, creations, and wisdom from everyone who has ever lived. You have access to this boundless resource through your mindset, prayer, inspiration, ideas, actions, and more.

The All holds the power to create anything, and *Brickhouse Mindset* is here to help you train your mind to tap into this resource intentionally, using it to your advantage as you create your best life.

Mindset, as defined by Stanford University, is the perspective you adopt for yourself. It is the lens through which you see the world, make decisions, and determine your course in life. It influences your daily actions and your long-term goals. Your mindset is not just a fleeting thought or attitude; it is a pervasive force that defines everything about you. It affects your expectations, and how you perceive your job, family, abilities, and most importantly how you see yourself.

Once you develop or obtain the mindset that supports your belief that you deserve the life of your desires or that you deserve your 'why', then your beliefs shape your actions. If you believe you deserve something and can achieve something, you are more likely to take the steps necessary to attain it. Even though you may not know the steps to take, they will come to you in gentle nudges and opened doors that you never knew were there. This is driven by *the Law of Inspired Action* which negates the *Law of Attraction* critics by encouraging purposeful steps toward your goals. According to this law, taking action aligns you with the energies and laws of manifestation, making your vision a reality.

It is imperative for you to first develop the mindset that you can have and deserve the life of your desires, and that there are universal forces, laws and alignments that will support your belief and bring them to you.

Without this core understanding, you may hesitate to take the steps necessary to bring your vision to life. This belief is the foundation of the cycle of achievement, the path to fulfilling your dreams and goals, and the power behind the self-fulfilling prophecy.

For example, I knew I had the skills and connections to create a website that promoted the musicians I loved, so I did the work to bring my vision to life. I expected success and was energized by the process. This is a simple illustration of "beginning with the end in mind," as explained in *The 7 Habits of Highly Effective People* (or any philosophy that teaches the importance of visualizing and believing in your end goal). You have to see and believe in the outcome before you can become or achieve it. This is a critical foundation for creating a lifestyle that aligns with your personal definition of success, whatever your goal or purpose may be.

It also serves as a reminder: if you believe that life is hard or that you'll never succeed, you're setting that expectation as your reality. Your life will reflect this belief until you decide to change it. By changing your mindset or your "truth" you create the power to change your outcomes.

Expectations play a significant role in our lives. If you expect people to treat you well, they often will. If you expect to excel at your job, you will put in the effort to do so. On the contrary, if you expect all men to cheat on you and treat you badly, then you most likely will mostly encounter men to fulfill your expectation, because this is what you believe. This is the frequency that you are working within and therefore you will attract things that are at the same frequency.

If you need something more scientific, then please read up on neuroplasticity. This refers to the brain's ability to reorganize itself by forming new neural connections throughout life. This means that our thoughts, habits, and experiences can physically change the structure of our brains and realign with the universal forces of our desires or the negative cycles we might unintentionally reinforce. The more we engage in particular thoughts or behaviors, the stronger those neural pathways become.

Science has proven that focused thought generates electromagnetic waves that resonate with the energy of your intentions, thus aligning with the universal frequencies. When you hold a thought for at least 17 seconds, as recommended by Abraham Hicks, you activate its vibrational frequency, harmonizing your energy with your desires and drawing them closer to you. This process doesn't just operate on a metaphysical level, it's rooted in and confirmed by science.

When you reinforce positive thoughts, those pathways grow stronger, making it easier to maintain an optimistic outlook. Engaging in joyful activities stimulates the brain to release neurotransmitters like dopamine, which not only boost positive emotions but also reinforce behaviors that attract more uplifting experiences. In essence, the power of belief is real and measurable, and the only true barrier to your goals is a lack of belief in yourself.

You Are a Powerful Manifesting Goddess.

You are already a powerful manifesting goddess, and the *Brickhouse Mindset* is here to help you harness your power to change your life for the better. Every day, you are manifesting, just look around. The life you're living, from the clothes you wear to the home you reside in, the job you have, the relationships you nurture, and the experiences you encounter, is a reflection of your choices and energy. Every item, every connection, every opportunity has been drawn into your orbit because, consciously or unconsciously, you aligned with their frequency. Whether it's your career, your health, your personal growth, or your dreams of love and abundance, everything in your life begins with the energy you put out into the world.

When you step into your power and become a master manifestor as I'm teaching you to become through *Brickhouse Mindset,* you align with your true desires and in partnership with Spirit become the co-creator of the life you've always envisioned. This is your journey to designing a life that resonates with your deepest dreams and ambitions, and to become the architect of your own destiny. You hold the blueprint; now it's time to design a destiny that resonates with your soul and fulfills your greatest potential.

Brickhouse Mindset is a framework, an owner's manual designed to teach you how to focus your mind on creating and living your best life. I'm simplifying a process that has been practiced and refined for centuries, breaking down key concepts to support you on your journey. I encourage you to explore the topics discussed in this book further, so you can deepen your connection to both the universe and yourself. For now, take these interpretations as a starting point, and dive deeper when you're ready.

As stated, your mindset dictates what you think you deserve. If you believe you deserve a better job, a healthier body, or a more fulfilling life, you are more likely to pursue those desires actively. It is crucial to foster beliefs that empower you rather than hold you back. Believing in your own desires, worthiness, abilities, and potential can open doors to opportunities and personal growth. Continuing to reshape your desires as you grow is the process of life.

Laying Bricks

You will never know everything, and your life experiences will continue to change and evolve, as will your goals and dreams. Your job is to strive to do and be your best so that you will enjoy the journey and live a fulfilled life.

In my Brickhouse Framework, detailed in the next chapter, I outline specific steps for you to take to help focus and curate your mind to support the work of your desires. Now that I hopefully have opened you up to the vastness of your mind, this universe and all that there is to help you manifest, I want you to fiercely comprehend the most important thing you must release in order to manifest.

Resistance

Equally as simple, but perhaps the hardest part to activate is the need to release resistance so that your manifestations can come into your reality. Resistance, or non-belief is an extremely limiting factor within manifestation. It can slow you down and prevent you from manifesting. As the saying goes, 'if you believe you will achieve', and if you do not believe, you will not achieve.

Releasing resistance is essential when it comes to manifesting your best life. Resistance arises from doubts, fears, or lingering beliefs that tell us we're not worthy or capable, and these energies work against the natural flow of abundance available to us. When we hold on to these resistant thoughts, it's like swimming against the current; it drains our energy, stirs up frustration, and keeps us from fully aligning with what we desire.

Imagine what it would feel like to let go of resistance, to trust the process, to feel worthy of your dreams, and to believe that the universe is working with you, not against you. When you release resistance, you allow yourself to move with the current of life rather than against it. You begin to open yourself up to receiving, recognizing opportunities, and feeling a deep sense of peace and confidence that what you desire is already on its way.

Letting go of resistance doesn't mean ignoring challenges or pretending everything is perfect. It means facing your doubts and limitations, accepting them for what they are, and choosing to believe anyway. Resistance often lives in our attachment to controlling every detail, the fear of failure, or the need to know every step of the journey. Releasing it involves embracing trust, trust in yourself, in the process, and in the universal laws that support your growth and fulfillment. By letting go of the need to control or force things to happen, you allow your desires to come to you in ways you may not have imagined.

As you release resistance, you cultivate a new state of mind, one that is open, receptive, and aligned with the energies of abundance, love, and possibility. You become free to take inspired action without the weight of fear or doubt holding you back. And as you practice releasing resistance, you'll find that your life begins to unfold in beautiful ways, drawing in experiences, people, and opportunities that resonate with your highest self. Embracing a life free from resistance allows you to manifest with ease, creating a reality that reflects the dreams, peace, and joy you hold within.

> The best way to move past any resistance is to focus on the goal and not the obstacle.

Laying Bricks

Once you start focusing on your goals, the solutions will start coming to you easier. You are training your mind to focus on the goal and ignore the illusions, confusion or fear. Remove their power because your goals are more important than what you think is blocking you. When you focus on the feelings the goal brings, you allow the solutions to vibrate towards you because you are on the same frequency of the goal achieved. The solutions may not come right away, but you start to see how much of your peace you disrupted by focusing on the obstacle and not the goal.

The *Brickhouse Mindset* is training you to develop new habits that will greatly benefit your life, so you must approach each change with patience with yourself as some of these changes are working to reprogram decades of habits and thought processes. Your goal is to develop a process or lifestyle that best enables you to achieve the life that you desire. When worry, resistance and challenges come, you now have a framework to remind you of where you may have fallen off track, and a process to help you continue forward with more peace.

Homework

This assignment is designed to help you apply the 12 Universal Laws to your life and learn practical steps to release resistance, so you can align with your desires and manifest the life of your dreams.

Step 1: Understanding the Laws in Your Life

Choose **three Universal Laws** (e.g., the Law of Attraction, the Law of Action, or the Law of Vibration) and reflect on how they currently apply to your life.

1. Write down one area of your life where you feel stuck or unfulfilled.
   - Example: career, relationships, health, or personal growth.

2. For each of the three chosen laws:
   - Briefly explain how this law can help you in that specific area.
   - Write down one action or mindset shift you can take to align with this law.

Example for the Law of Vibration:
- **Current Situation:** I feel stuck in my career because I doubt my abilities.
- **Application:** The Law of Vibration reminds me that my energy attracts similar energy. By focusing on gratitude for the skills I have, I can raise my vibration to attract better opportunities.
- **Action:** Start a gratitude journal and write three things I appreciate about my career skills every day.

Step 2: Identifying and Releasing Resistance
1. Write down a specific desire you want to manifest.
   - Be as detailed as possible. For example: "I want a fulfilling career where I feel valued, earn $100,000 a year, and have work-life balance."

2. Reflect on what's holding you back from manifesting this desire.
   - What are your doubts, fears, or limiting beliefs?
   - Are there habits, people, or situations adding resistance to your progress?

3. Use the following questions to help you identify resistance:
    - Am I focused more on the problem than the solution?
    - Do I feel worthy of receiving what I desire?
    - Am I clinging to control or afraid of the unknown?

Step 3: Letting Go and Creating Space for Alignment

1. **Reframe Your Resistance:**
   For each limitation or fear you identified in Step 2, write a positive affirmation or belief that counters it.

    - Example:
        - Resistance: "I don't have enough experience to pursue my dream job."
        - Reframe: "I am constantly growing and learning. My unique skills and potential make me perfect for the opportunities I seek."

2. **Visualize Without Resistance:**
   Spend 5-10 minutes each day visualizing your desire as if it has already happened. Use vivid detail, and most importantly, focus on the feeling it brings.
    - Imagine holding the job offer letter, seeing the zeros in your bank account, or feeling the joy of a healthy relationship.

3. **Action Steps to Release Resistance:**
   Choose one practice to incorporate daily for the next week to release resistance. Options include:
    - **Meditation:** Focus on your breath and visualize letting go of any tension.
    - **Journaling:** Write about your ideal life without judgment or overthinking.

- **Physical Release:** Engage in yoga, exercise, or a calming walk to shift stagnant energy.

Step 4: Reflection and Accountability
At the end of the week, answer the following:
1. What shifts did you notice in your mindset or energy?
2. Did you take steps that aligned with the Universal Laws you focused on?
3. Were you able to release resistance and feel more at ease about your desire?
4. What can you do to continue building on this progress?

Remember: Manifestation is an ongoing journey, and releasing resistance is a practice. The more you align with your desires and trust the process, the closer you are to creating the life you dream of. You've got this, Brickhouse!

- Chapter 5 -

The Brickhouse Mindset Phase I

The Framework for Curating your Thoughts and Programming for Success

Brickhouse Mindset Shift: I am the gatekeeper of my thoughts; I choose peace over worry. My energy is rooted in the joy of the present moment.

Let's get cozy and explore what makes the *Brickhouse Mindset* a game-changer. This is where the magic begins, where you take control of your thoughts and create the foundation for a happier, more fulfilling life. The Brickhouse Mindset is a two-phase framework designed to help you manifest your desires with intention and clarity.

In the first phase, we focus on curating the thoughts that occupy your mind, aligning them with the life and experiences you want to attract. This is crucial because, as we've uncovered, the key to drawing your desires into reality is aligning your energy with them. When your mind not only envisions your dreams but truly believes you deserve them, the universe responds in kind. In this chapter, we'll focus on aligning your mindset to make sure it's working *for* you and not against you.

Once your mind is aligned, we'll move into the next phase: aligning your plan. Because the dream is only the beginning, the actions you take will bring it to life.

Step 1. Code Switch

Brickhouse Mindset Shift: I am the gatekeeper of my thoughts; I choose peace over worry.

> To change your life, you have got to start with your thoughts.

It is all about tweaking your mindset, reshaping how you see yourself, your experiences, and what you truly desire. Sounds like a lofty goal, right? But it is entirely achievable, and here's how.

Our thoughts are the creators of our reality. If you are constantly feeding your mind with worry, self-doubt or the ills of life, that's precisely what you'll attract. You will stay at a negative frequency. The *Brickhouse Mindset* begins with a simple yet profound skill, mastering your thoughts and feelings to vibrate at a higher frequency.

Now, here is the core skill that will change your life. Whenever worry, doubt, fear, darkness or self-sabotaging thought sneak into your mind, do not dwell on them. Instead, gently push them away, take some deep breaths and replace them with what I like to call a 'Passion Pic', and hold your thoughts there for about 20 seconds. This foundational practice is the basis for finding peace in the next moment.

The Brickhouse Mindset Phase I

The purpose is to pull you out of the negative frequency that you are currently vibing with in this funky state, and to find peace in the next moment by raising your vibration to that of your desires, what you love or something that makes you feel good, and to attract from this frequency.

The more you do this, the easier it will become, and you will start to utilize this as a way to navigate the stress, worry and confusion of life, by releasing its grip on your mind. It will become easier to acknowledge when you need to Code Switch because you will start to realize when you are lost in your worrisome or angry thoughts and know that you need to shift.

The Passion Pic

Imagine something that instantly warms your heart and makes you smile; something you love or desire. It could be anything, the smile from your sweet baby, a clean house, vacationing on a yacht, or maybe it's the success of your business, a dream lover, or anything that brings you joy. Use this image to instantly shift your focus to something that makes you feel good, when you are feeling low or focused on worry or the past.

This isn't just daydreaming it is about utilizing your imagination to redirect your energy towards what makes you feel better in the next moment and align with the frequency of your desires. Remember, whatever you put your attention towards is what you are creating. I have Passion Pics that instantly make me feel good or others that help me refocus on my dreams, and I pop them in my head frequently during the day depending on the need of the moment. Use this technique as your go to response whenever you feel worry or fear about something. If I am thinking about the hurt from a past lover, I immediately pivot to being on the beach with my new love. If I am thinking about my current challenges in life, I envision myself speaking to millions of you at a podium, accepting my awards, or being interviewed on the top television stations nationally.

Your Goal is to Vibrate High with the Things You Desire.

The goal here is to feel better in the moment, to shift your focus from what is bringing you down to what lifts you up. Your goal is a high vibration remember! To vibrate with the things that you desire and will better your life. Negative thoughts sap your energy and hinder your progress, so we are flipping the script. By cultivating a habit of replacing worry with these Passion Pics, you start to become more present with the current moment and free up more mental space for the things that really matter. Once you return to life after focusing on the Passion Pic, you feel better in the next moment, which is progress.

We spend so much time worrying about the past, and our problems, that we are not enjoying our present moments or creating the solutions. Worry is not helping anything. It is in fact bringing down your vibration and attracting more things to worry about. Our goal is to focus on the present moment and vibrate with what makes you feel good.

The Brickhouse Mindset Phase I

Especially in the beginning, this may be challenging, but when you catch yourself, immediately push out the thought, take a deep breath and focus on something that makes you feel good, then better, then great. This new and great vibration puts you back in frequency to attract the thoughts, actions, opportunities, and feelings that you need in order to attract and manifest the life and experiences that you want.

Release the thought, repeat the Passion Pic, release the thought, repeat the Passion Pic, repeat, repeat, repeat.

Just like any human, those doubts, fears and frustrations will come up every day; but by getting into the practice of instantly releasing them, they will come less frequently, and when they do come you will know how to push them out of your head and focus on what feels better. This is how you learn to reduce worrying, re-living pain or living in fear and regret. You simply stop focusing on them.

Your goal is to be present in the now moments while being optimistic about the future you are creating in peace and appreciation. Living in the past is the biggest thief of peace. Remember, life is simple but not easy, but it can become easier. By simply adopting this new mindset your life will open up in ways unimagined. The weight of fear and despair will lighten and make room for love, accomplishment and peace.

I want to be clear here, I am not telling you to ignore your sadness or heavy feelings because you are entitled to them, and these are natural parts of life. Life as I said will have its ups and downs, it's on a cycle. When something happens to you and you are pained, hurt or disappointed, you will feel it and there is no way getting around it. This is natural and I am by no means want to rob you of your feelings and what you can learn from them.

When it comes to grief, particularly in moments of deep despair, seeking support from qualified professionals may be essential to help you regain balance. It's crucial to move through your emotions, especially trauma, as unprocessed pain can linger and manifest as mental or physical ailments. This is where self-care and practices to clear negative energy become vital to your healing process. While honoring your feelings is important, there will come a time when you'll seek peace and feel ready to move forward with your life, embracing the next chapter with renewed strength.

My main point is that worrying about your worries does not bring solutions.

This only brings more worry and ill feelings to your mind and life. In addition, our worries rarely manifest in the way that we worried about, and many times we are focused on the worst-case scenario, instead of being focused on our desired outcome which is the most beneficial. Vibing with and focusing on your desired outcomes, feelings and life experiences are the creators of these good and great things and bring the love and lightness we need in life. You do not even have to worry about how those solutions will come, just know they will come, and when they do, act on them.

The *Brickhouse Mindset* offers a powerful path for women to take control of their mental health, providing a framework to process emotions, restore balance, and build a life aligned with their deepest desires. It is my heartfelt prayer that Spirit guides every woman who feels lost under the weight of life's challenges to embrace this framework, empowering her to rise above those burdens without needing institutions or medication. This mindset is a lifeline, designed to help reclaim your strength, peace, and joy.

This practice is a powerful tool to dismiss the worry and negativity that disrupt your peace of mind. It helps you break free from the cycle of pain, depression, distractions, gossip, self-criticism, and other habits that keep you stuck focusing on what you don't want instead of what you do want. These patterns lower your vibration, leaving you feeling drained and engaging in actions that don't align with the life you ultimately desire.

Remember, no one is harder on you than you, but don't add to that burden by criticizing yourself for not always staying upbeat or focused. Life is full of highs and lows and navigating them is part of the journey. By incorporating the Passion Pic and the practices outlined in this book, you will find it easier to move through those moments, shifting your focus to joy, peace, and purpose. Over time, your life will become more fulfilling, more balanced, and more aligned with your dreams, allowing you to accomplish more and cultivate a deep sense of gratitude.

The ultimate goal of the Passion Pic is to reset your energetic feeling so that you are vibrating at a higher frequency and can attract better feelings and more better feelings and ultimately the feelings and lifestyle that you desire.

The things that you want are most likely at a high vibration because they make you feel good. That great career, family, accomplishment, healthy body and relationship are desired because they make you feel good right? So, in efforts to attract those great things, you must vibrate with them, so your vibe must remain high so that you are aligned.

It is that simple and that deep. In order to align and attract your desires, you must vibrate with them, so the more things you can do during the day to feel good, feel accomplished and at peace will attract more good things and feelings and ultimately your desired lifestyle.

The Power of Visualization

As you grow more comfortable pivoting to your Passion Pic, supercharge the process by immersing yourself fully in its visualization. Don't just think about your Passion Pic, experience it vividly in your mind. Whether it's your dream house, a loving relationship, your ideal career, or financial freedom, bring it to life with as much detail as possible. Feel the warmth of the room, hear the laughter, imagine the kiss, and believe in it.

Building on the teachings of Abraham Hicks, focus on your Passion Pic for at least 17 seconds to activate its frequency. To make this easier, envision a short mental movie where you see yourself already living your desired reality. Picture the scene: Who is there, celebrating with you? What does the scenery look like? What are you wearing? What are you doing? Let yourself fully embody the joy, excitement, and fulfillment of that moment. Smile, let the warmth flood your body, and feel it as if it's happening now.

To amplify this practice, revisit your Passion Pic at least three times daily, morning, midday, and just before bed to anchor your focus and realign your energy. Numbers hold significant power, and 3 is known as a magical accelerator worth exploring further. By repeatedly tuning into the feeling of your Passion Pic, you raise your vibration and align yourself with the life you're working to manifest.

My Dear Brickhouse, your visualizations and the feeling of living in the dream fulfilled are the creators of your future. The more detail and attention you can give to your dreams increases your attraction to them. You're not just wishing for them; you are aligning your vibration with them. If visualization is challenging for you, don't stay focused on the specifics. If it is easier for you to write or speak to your dreams, do that and know that what Spirit has for you is greater than you can imagine. As you grow, your vision will sharpen and change anyway. The important thing is maintaining the feeling of your dream fulfilled and vibrating high. This is a process of manifestation.

Incorporate visualization into your meditation and prayer practice. I usually start out my meditation sessions with a prayer giving thanks to The Most High for all of my blessings and for all that I want as if I already have it. I then visualize my Passion Pics, and then go into silent meditation for at least 20 minutes. If you are just beginning a meditation practice, start with the intention of a three-minute meditation and build from there. A good meditation session that lasts 10 minutes can yield about 3 minutes of pure mental silence, so don't be hard on yourself because your mind wanders. It happens to everyone, and sometimes inspiration and answers come in during meditation.

I encourage you to develop your own practices and understanding when it comes to your spirituality.

What I'm sharing here is simply an example of mine, which has evolved over time and will continue to grow as I do. Part of my nighttime routine involves visualizing my Passion Pics and intentionally cultivating positive feelings before bed. This practice helps me align with peace and set the tone for restorative sleep.

It's equally important to create a calming environment by turning off electronics or engaging with something soothing to your soul, such as relaxing music, meditation, or uplifting content. Avoid watching the news, true crime, or anything heavy right before bed. These thoughts can linger in your subconscious and may affect your dreams, mood, and energy upon waking. Instead, focus on feeding your mind with positivity and peace as you transition into sleep.

Your subconscious mind is the mind that is still aware while you sleep. Listening to self-help books, affirmations, meditation music or binaural beats while you sleep is another good practice. Even though you are sleeping, your brain is not and is still absorbing and thinking while you are sleeping. Information, inspiration and plans may come to you in dreams or shortly after waking.

The Brickhouse Mindset Phase I

Do it with Optimism

The key to manifesting and mastering this mindset shift is daily practice. Every time you find yourself down the rabbit hole with worry, immediately steer your focus toward your Passion Pic and what feels better in the moment. With consistent effort, you will find yourself naturally gravitating toward optimism and not being stuck in sadness, lack or the past. I am careful to not say positivity, because what is meant for good is always somehow skewed for confusion; and positivity is a trigger word for some. Optimism is actually the best word to use any way. You want to look to life with the optimism of having better than you expect. You will start to appreciate the moments of peace, joyful experiences, great music and kindness that you previously did not value as much. You want to embrace the feeling of optimism, like all is well and getting better.

Remember, this is not about empty affirmations or quick fixes. It is a journey to reshape your thoughts, your knowings, and ultimately, your life. It is about claiming the happiness and fulfillment you deserve, one thought at a time. The more that you envision the dream, experience the love, achieve the success, or whatever makes you feel fantabulous, the easier you will manifest it!

Visualize & Release

Your goal again is to embrace the feeling so that you can create from a higher vibration, not to only focus on what you want all day and get angry with yourself when you are feeling low. As you visualize you are detailing your desires and asking Spirit to create the best possible options for you. Then release it and go about your day finding and doing things that can bring joy and peace in each day. As you start to see better experiences and opportunities enter your life, you will see that what Spirit delivered for you is beyond what you can imagine. That is because it has the power of the entire Universe to create from and it knows the best possible solutions for your desires. All you have to do is ask for it, expect it, find peace in the next moment and acknowledge the blessings when they come.

Do not stay focused incessantly all day, every day on what you want, because you are not allowing room for the desired outcome to arrive in peace, you are trying to force it. We rarely get what we want exactly when or in the exact way we want it because things take time to align and come together. Creation takes time and life is a journey. You can miss out on the joy of life if you are only focused on what is not currently here. Our timing is not Spirit's timing.

> If you are concerned or upset about how long it is taking for something to happen, you are still not in a state of peace nor knowing that what you desire will come.

I absolutely started manifesting my new life in Atlanta starting about 3 years before publishing this book. After my divorce, I needed a change big time and developed a strong desire to move to Atlanta. I visited often for work and to visit a lover (that we will discuss later) and fell in love with the city. All day I would daydream about Atlanta. I often returned home with different things to establish connections with Atlanta. I bought a key chain, a t-shirt and finally about 1 month before I moved, I brought home some dirt that I dug up to take my manifestation rituals to the next level. License plates and regular mentions on TV, the radio, etc. followed me around. I met an assembly line of people and new family members from Atlanta. Then, after achieving Chairman's Club at my job, I was offered a promotion in Atlanta! I knew this was Spirit ordering my steps!

I encountered enormous obstacles, seemingly preventing my move, but the universe, my desire, focused energy and many, many miracles conspired together to enable me to move. Now, I am here, writing this owner's manual sitting thankfully in my new home in Atlanta. I should have been here decades ago.

Homework
Step 1: Identify Negative Patterns
1. **Reflection Exercise:**
    - Spend 10-15 minutes reflecting on your recent thoughts and feelings. Write down any recurring worries, fears, or self-sabotaging beliefs.
    - For each one, note how it makes you feel. (E.g., "I can't achieve my goals" makes me feel defeated.)
    - For every entry write a note that details how you wish to feel. (I.e., "I achieve my goals with ease joy and grace.")
    - Throughout the week, keep a small notebook or use the notes app on your phone to jot down moments

when you catch yourself spiraling into negativity. Write what triggered the thought and how it affected your mood.

Step 2: Create Your Passion Pics
1. **Visualization Creation:**
    - Identify three Passion Pics that immediately uplift you. These can be:
        - A cherished memory (e.g., a trip to the beach).
        - A future dream (e.g., living in your dream home or holding your award-winning book).
        - A symbolic image (e.g., a serene lake representing peace).

2. **Detail the Feeling:**
    - Write a paragraph about each Passion Pic. Describe it in vivid detail, including colors, smells, sounds, and feelings. Immerse yourself in it as if you are experiencing it now.

Step 3: Evaluate Progress
1. **Weekly Check-In:**
    - After a week, review your journal entries. Reflect on these questions:

- Did Code Switching become easier with practice?
- Have you noticed any shifts in your energy or mindset?
- Are you starting to feel more optimistic about your goals and desires?

Remember:
- Be patient with yourself. Code Switching is a skill that develops with consistent practice.
- This isn't about perfection; it's about progress. Celebrate every moment you choose to shift your energy and elevate your vibration.
- Keep this framework close and continue to refine it as you grow. Your Passion Pics and visualizations will evolve alongside you.

Step 2: Feed

Brickhouse Mindset Shift: What I consume shapes my reality. I feed my mind with all the good that I desire.

Now my dear Brickhouse, we delve into the importance of feeding your temple body with the mental and emotional food that will help you become your best self. If your goal is to lose weight or simply live a healthier life, it is obvious that you must start by adjusting what you are eating, exercising and seeking out a lifestyle that supports your goals, but it is more than just that.

Curate your Media

Creating your best life is about more than just setting goals and working towards them, it's about cultivating an environment that supports your growth, well-being, and success. One of the most impactful yet often overlooked elements of this environment is the information you consume. Every day, we are bombarded with media, television, music, and conversations that can either uplift us or drain our energy. If you're on a journey to create a fulfilling and purposeful life, it's crucial to curate the information you take in. As Brickhouses, it's important to know that the content we allow into our minds can either propel us toward our dreams or hold us back.

Think of your mind as a garden: what you plant and water will grow. If you fill your mind with negative news, gossip, and toxic media, you're planting seeds of doubt, fear, and distraction. But when you consciously choose to feed your mind with knowledge, wisdom, and empowering content, you plant seeds of growth, focus, and optimism. The information you consume shapes your thoughts, and your thoughts shape your actions. To achieve your goals, you must be intentional about what you allow into your mind and feed it with good information.

Start by assessing the media you consume. Are you watching television shows that inspire you or ones that drain your energy? Are you following social media accounts that uplift and motivate you, or are you constantly exposed to negativity and comparison? Take a look at the books, podcasts, and music that fill your days. Are they aligned with the life you're working to create, or do they distract you from your purpose?

As Brickhouses, our goals require us to be sharp, knowledgeable, and mentally resilient.

> We must fill our minds with information that brings us joy, enhance our skills, deepen our understanding, and fuel our ambition.

Whether it's learning new strategies to grow your business, staying updated on topics relevant to your career, or consuming content that keeps you motivated, your media choices should be a reflection of the life you're building. This is how you stay ahead, informed, and ready to take action.

Protecting Your Energy and Mindset

What we consume doesn't just affect our knowledge base, it also deeply impacts our emotional energy and mindset. If you are constantly exposed to negative conversations, fear-based news, or toxic social media, your energy will reflect that. You might feel anxious, pessimistic, or even hopeless about your goals. On the other hand, when you surround yourself with joyful and empowering content and uplifting conversations, your mindset shifts. You feel more optimistic, energized, and capable of achieving greatness.

One of the keys to success is maintaining a positive and focused mindset. The energy you bring to your work and relationships will determine the quality of the results you achieve. This is why it's so important to be intentional about the information you allow into your space. When you start curating your media and conversations, you create a protective barrier around your mental and emotional health. You give yourself the gift of joy, optimism, focus, and drive, which are essential to reaching your goals.

My dear Brickhouse, if you want to live powerful, joyful, and successful lives, you must fill your days with content that reflects those values. Choose to follow influencers who inspire you, read books that challenge your thinking, listen to audiobooks and podcasts that expand your knowledge, and engage in conversations that uplift you. The more you align your media intake with your goals and what feels good, the more supported and empowered you will feel on your journey.

Surround Yourself with Supportive Conversations

Another powerful shift happens when you change the conversations around you. The people you talk to on a daily basis can either build you up or tear you down. If you're constantly surrounded by individuals who gossip, complain, or focus on negativity, it's easy to get pulled into that energy. But when you intentionally engage with people who are positive, ambitious, and supportive, you elevate your mindset and reinforce your goals.

Take note of the people in your circle. Are they rooting for your success? Do they speak life into your dreams and encourage you when things get tough? Or are they more focused on drama and negativity? As a Brickhouse, you must surround yourself with conversations that match the energy you want to maintain. Seek out those who challenge you to be better, who inspire you to think bigger, and who hold you accountable to your goals. Positive and supportive conversations will fuel your motivation and help you stay focused when distractions arise.

Changing your feeds is not just a one-time action, it's an ongoing practice of conscious consumption. It's about consistently choosing what aligns with the person you are becoming and the life you are building. This is your life, and you have the power to decide what you consume. The more you do this, you will start to weed out the influences, television shows and music that no longer resonate with your frequencies as you rise towards your goals.

Here are some takeaways to help you change your feeds and curate the information you consume.

- **Audit Your Current Media Intake**: Review the television shows, podcasts, books, and social media accounts you regularly engage with. Identify which ones align with your goals and which ones may be distracting or draining your energy.
- **Unfollow Negative Accounts**: On social media, unfollow any accounts that promote negativity, comparison, or gossip. Replace them with accounts that share positivity,

inspiration, and knowledge that align with your personal and professional goals.

- **Set Daily Content Goals**: Allocate specific time each day for consuming content that supports your growth, such as listening to an educational podcast, reading a book related to your goals, or watching a motivational video.
- **Limit News Consumption**: Set boundaries around your intake of news, especially fear-based or sensationalized media. Focus on credible sources and limit your news exposure to specific times during the day.
- **Engage in Uplifting Conversations**: Surround yourself with positive people who support your ambitions. Seek out conversations that inspire growth, positivity, and new ideas. Avoid engaging in gossip or negativity.
- **Follow Thought Leaders and Experts**: Find and follow thought leaders, influencers, and experts in your field who share valuable insights and knowledge. Engage with their content to stay informed and inspired.
- **Curate an Educational Playlist**: Create a playlist of podcasts, audiobooks, or videos that expand your knowledge and motivate you. Listen to these while commuting or during downtime.
- **Join Supportive Communities**: Participate in online forums, groups, or networks that are focused on personal growth, goal achievement, or professional development. Share and

engage with like-minded individuals who are on similar journeys.

One trick that has greatly increased the content that I am able to absorb is that I listen to YouTube videos and audiobooks that align with my goals while I work out. I am learning while I am exercising! Merging two things that most find hard to make time for has improved every aspect of my life. I will say that this alone accelerated my ascension and results tremendously.

Step 3: Affirm

Brickhouse Mindset Shift: My words have power. What I say and write is so.

Now, let's dive into the encouraging world of affirmations and journaling. Affirmations are like your daily personal pep talk from the Universe. They are positive, intentional statements that help you reinforce empowering beliefs and shape your mindset. They're usually written or spoken in the present tense, as if the desired outcome or quality is already true. For example, "I am worthy of success," or "I am abundant in all areas of my life." By repeating affirmations regularly, you condition your mind to focus on positive beliefs and possibilities, aligning your thoughts with your goals and dreams.

The power of affirmations lies in their ability to counter negative self-talk or limiting beliefs. Each time you affirm a positive statement, you're helping to rewire your brain, creating new neural pathways that support your growth and well-being. When repeated consistently, affirmations can influence how you perceive yourself and your potential, boost your confidence, and even improve your outlook on life. This simple practice can increase self-awareness and resilience, helping you overcome obstacles with a mindset rooted in optimism and self-empowerment.

My Dear Brickhouse, your affirmations are programming your brain to believe and attract your desires.

Words are spells, that is why it is called spelling. I will tip toe into the etymology of words, but this whole book is focused on how crucial it is that you start to choose your thoughts, words, and actions carefully. When you speak/think words, you are placing your mind on the frequency of your words/thoughts and attracting them to you. So, by reciting and writing affirmations of your desires, you are programing your mind, your experiences, and The All to work together to make them happen. Some that I have been reciting either aloud or in my head daily include:

- I am 100% healthy and well.
- I am the love and light of God.
- I Am protected by the love & the light of God.
- All that is for my highest good is delivered to me with ease, joy & grace.
- I Am a powerful manifesting goddess.
- I help millions of women become their best selves.

The Brickhouse Mindset Phase I

These affirmations have been my daily companions for years, and they have helped shape my current reality. I often recite them along with my Passion Pics to distract my mind when I am challenged and need encouragement. It is important for you to develop and write affirmations that not only inspire you and pull you out of dark places, but also support your goals and dreams. If you are working on shedding weight, your affirmations may look like:

- I am thriving at my most beautiful and ideal weight.
- Weight sheds easily off my body.
- I enjoy eating healthily.
- I am excited seeing the changes happening within my body!

Or if you are working on developing your business, some affirmations may include:

- I am the owner of a stable and financially abundant business.
- My business sustains my family for generations.
- People are eager to pay for my services on a regular basis.
- My income increases daily.
- I attract trustworthy and supportive team members that help me build my business.

The goal is not to have the perfect affirmations, it is to experience the feelings the affirmations give you as they program your beliefs and align your actions. Reciting your affirmations put you on a positive vibration and ultimately within the frequency of your desires. They work to instill in your soul the belief that you are, and your will is done with the blessings of The Divine.

As you know, a key to manifestation is to feel that you are or already have what you want. So, with all that you do, say your affirmations with peace, love and optimistic excitement! To keep that beautiful energy circulating throughout your day, smile and say your affirmations in the morning, before you go to bed, in the shower, or even put them up on your desk at work. Post sticky notes on your mirrors and recite them, or download apps that pop them up on your phone throughout the day to inspire you. Follow social media that promote affirmations that speak to you. Use technology and your creativity to incorporate affirmations into your daily life.

I say mine all day, and I often find myself saying them while I am daydreaming, doing dishes or something that allows me to zen out and be in a state of peace. The more you repeat them and see them, the more they become ingrained in your subconscious mind. Whether you say your affirmations out loud or within your head will vibrate at the same frequency but saying them out loud may make the vibration stronger. Google and especially search Pinterest for affirmation inspirations and make them your own. Work with an intention to say your affirmations at least 3 specific times a day.

Choose Your Words

The significance of choosing one's words has more power than you may realize. Words are not mere expressions but potent tools that shape our reality and influence the unfolding of our lives. Every word we utter carries the power to manifest our desires or invite adversity into our existence. Think about the words that were spoken to you as a child, and how they may have majorly influenced your life in a beneficial way or crushed your dreams entirely.

Our words are like seeds sown into the fertile soil of the universe. They take root and grow, eventually bearing fruit. If we sow positive, affirming words, we reap a bountiful harvest of joy, abundance, and success. Conversely, when we allow negative, self-defeating language to escape our lips, we are claiming limitations and struggles. To manifest our desires, we must not only choose our words carefully but also cultivate a mindset aligned with our aspirations. Replace doubt with faith, fear with courage, and lack with abundance in both our thoughts and expressions.

When you speak about your desires, speak as if you already have them.

Do not say "I will, or it will", speak as if you already have it. That day in the future will never come if you keep saying it will come or it is on its way. It is here for you now and give thanks for it. If you *will* become a successful author, homeowner, or better parent, you are always speaking of sometime in the future. This is why it is important to use the term I AM.

I AM is now and confirmation that it is done.

I AM successful, I AM abundant, I Have achieved whatever I Am working on. Assume the feeling that you have already achieved the dream so that you will vibrate with it and draw it closer to you. When you have that feeling, it activates and amplifies the manifestation!

By speaking as if you are already what you desire, you will realize that you are creating it now and start to see your accomplishments in real life. You will recognize how far you have come, how much you have improved and how many things start to flow to you to help you along your journey. Life is a journey. If you are only awaiting some future win, you are missing the beautiful reminders along the way. You are missing the small wins, ignoring the daily events to be grateful for, and not experiencing the peace in the moment. Draw what you wish into your presence by declaring it so and acknowledging it.

While we are at it, erase words like 'can't' and 'try' from your vocabulary. You can do anything you put your mind to and the less you use the word can't, the stronger your manifestation powers will grow. Speak life into what you want instead of what you do not think you can have or do.

Instead of saying what you can't do, say:
- what you prefer to do
- what you need more time/practice or support to do
- what you are working through the difficulties of

Do you see how changing that word provides more clarity and direction on what is possible or needed instead of what you think you cannot do?

Do not try, simply do. You are not trying, you are doing or attempting to do. Using the phrase "I'm trying" can sometimes imply a lack of commitment or confidence in achieving a goal. It can leave room for doubt and suggests that success is uncertain. A Brickhouse claims success because she is making it so. Focus on what you are doing.

Instead of saying "I'm trying," consider using more assertive and empowering language to convey your commitment and determination. Say:

- I'm working on...
- I'm committed to...
- I'm focused on...
- I'm taking steps to...

The language you use, and the intent is important, so choose more assertive language, so that you can get in the habit of cultivating a more positive mindset with your words, reinforce your determination, and increase your likelihood of success in achieving your goals.

I also stopped saying things like "Good Morning", "I'm tired" "I'm sick", "I'm broke" or talking about doing something "to death", etc. Morning sounds like mourning, and regardless of your intent, the Universe is responding to the resonance of the word. The alignment of the letters in your words activate vibrations that align with the frequencies of ancient energy and understanding. I replaced these phrases with "Hello" or "Good Day", "I am going to rest", "I am healing", etc. You never want to call in brokenness or a lack of finances, so you can say "my money is growing" or "that is not in my budget right now" instead.

As I got deeper into my mastery of manifestation powers, I started finding more words and phrases that are woven into our everyday dialogue that were calling death or darkness, and I now make a conscious effort to use more edifying words. This may sound like I am going way too deep with this, but if you think about how often we use these terms, the power of words and the importance of resonating with your desires, your resistance will fade as your alignment grows.

Another thing to think about is when someone asks how we're doing, it's all too common to respond with a list of our problems or to speak about life as if it's a constant struggle. We may find ourselves venting about stress, frustrations, or what's going wrong without even realizing the impact it has on our mindset. Speaking about life in this way not only reinforces negative energy within us, but it also spreads that energy outward, affecting how others perceive and experience their interactions with us.

Imagine how different things would feel if, instead, we focused on what's going well. Shifting the focus to the good in our lives, even small moments of joy or gratitude, change the entire tone of our day. When we answer with something positive, like an accomplishment we're proud of, a kind gesture we experienced, or simply a feeling of gratitude, we reinforce these uplifting feelings within ourselves. This doesn't mean we ignore challenges or pretend everything is perfect; rather, it's about consciously choosing to give energy to the parts of life that fill us with joy, peace, and appreciation.

By speaking about the good, we invite more of it into our lives. This habit shapes our perspective, allowing us to see opportunities and solutions instead of just obstacles. When we answer with positivity, we're also creating a ripple effect; the energy we put into the world comes back to us, and the person we're speaking to feels uplifted as well. Gradually, this practice builds a mindset rooted in gratitude and optimism, making it easier to see our lives in a positive light.

The next time someone asks how you are, pause and think about something good in your life, no matter how small. Share that. Speak about your goals, your progress, the things you're grateful for, or simply that you're working toward a better version of yourself. By choosing to focus on the positive, you're setting the foundation for a life that feels lighter, brighter, and more aligned with the joy and abundance you deserve.

We have the power to rewrite our stories by consciously selecting words that affirm our goals and dreams. By doing so, we establish a harmonious resonance with the universe, attracting the circumstances and opportunities that propel us toward our desires. The importance of choosing our words goes beyond mere communication, it is a profound act of co-creation with the universe. It is a reminder that our words shape our destiny, and by embracing positivity, faith, and intention in our language, we become architects of a life filled with limitless possibilities.

Journaling

In today's digital age, we often underestimate the profound impact of putting pen to paper. But trust me, it is a game-changer. Writing down your daily thoughts, goals, and affirmations is an art form, a connection, and another creative act with the Universe.

When you journal, you create a space to reflect on your thoughts, clarify your desires, and set intentions that align with the life you want to create.

Incorporating journaling into your daily practice allows you to keep track of your progress, setbacks, and triumphs, and can be one of your most powerful tools for manifesting your best self. This documentation of your life allows you to reflect on your experiences, turning each entry into a powerful tool for growth and self-discovery. By recording what you go through, the highs, lows, and everything in between, you create a map of your life that allows you to see patterns, lessons, and moments of resilience. This reflection helps you realize how far you've come, which can be incredibly motivating and affirming as you pursue your dreams.

Documenting your experiences also helps you process your emotions, giving you a safe space to work through complex feelings and gain clarity on your thoughts. Writing about your challenges can reveal insights and solutions you may not have seen otherwise, while celebrating your successes helps reinforce positive habits and boosts self-confidence. Over time, journaling helps you build self-awareness, showing you how certain choices and attitudes shape your life and highlighting the changes you can make to align with your best self.

You can also use your journal to identify and release limiting beliefs that may be holding you back. As you write, be honest with yourself about any doubts, fears, or negative self-talk that arise. Acknowledge these thoughts without judgment, and then reframe them with empowering statements. For example, if you feel unworthy of success, write about why you deserve to achieve your goals and the steps you're taking to reach them.

You can also use what is known as scripting, as a powerful tool to support you in manifesting the life you want, by writing as if your dreams have already come true. While journaling helps you explore your current experiences and emotions, **scripting takes things a step further by guiding you to write about your future as if it has already happened.** Scripting helps you align your thoughts, emotions, and energy with the frequency of your goals, allowing you to see, feel, and embody the life you're creating.

Start by setting aside some quiet time in a comfortable space. Grab your journal and begin to write a story about your ideal life, as if you're already living it. Use present tense statements like "I am," "I have," and "I feel" to make it real. Describe a rundown of your day or ideal life in detail. Where are you going, what are you doing, what are you wearing and who is with you. How do you feel, believing that you have achieved your goals? Picture the people around you, the places you go, how you carry yourself, and how fulfilling each moment feels. Let yourself become fully immersed in this vision as you write, feeling the joy, peace, and excitement of living this life right now. This simple act of aligning your energy with the vibration of your desires helps to attract the opportunities, relationships, and experiences that match what you've scripted.

Scripting and journaling are closely connected because both allow you to reflect on your desires, clarify your goals, and channel your thoughts into powerful words that shape your reality. These ongoing rituals help you stay aligned with your intentions, release resistance, and consistently nurture the plans for your best life. With each page you write, you're stepping closer to becoming the woman you dream of being, living the life you deserve.

Homework

In this homework assignment, I invite you to explore the profound impact of your words, the practice of affirmations, and the benefits of journaling.

- Write down 5 or more personal affirmations that reflect positive changes or goals you want to manifest in your life. Ensure that these affirmations are specific, present-tense, and framed in a positive light. For example, "I am confident in my abilities and attract success effortlessly."

    - Incorporate your chosen affirmations into your daily routine. Repeat them in the morning, throughout the day, and before bedtime.
    - Keep a record of any noticeable changes in your life, thoughts, feelings, or actions as a result of using these affirmations.

- Write a list of 4 or more words or phrases that you can work to eliminate from your vocabulary and what you will replace them with. Stay mindful and actively switch these words throughout the day.

- If you are not already doing so, begin a journal to document your thoughts, feelings, and experiences as you read the *Brickhouse Mindset*, with an intention to do so on a daily basis.

Here are some journal prompts to aide your writing:
- Reflect on your journey with the *Brickhouse Mindset*. What aspects of the book are resonating deeply with you, and which ones are you finding challenging or conflicting? Be honest and explore any resistance you may be experiencing.
- Take a moment to list three things you're genuinely grateful for today and everyday moving forward.
- Outline your strategies for maintaining and reinforcing your new *Brickhouse Mindset*. How can you stay committed to your growth and continue embodying the principles outlined in the book?

Step 4: Believe

Brickhouse Mindset Shift: Belief is my superpower; when I believe it is already done.

Let us delve into one of the foundational bricks of the *Brickhouse Mindset*, Belief. Belief is the magic wand that can turn your dreams into reality. It is the fuel that propels you forward, even when the road gets tough. But belief isn't just a fleeting thought or a wishful notion, it's a deep, unwavering conviction. A knowing that what you desire is not only possible but inevitable.

How do you cultivate this conviction? Through repetition and aligned action. When you consistently reinforce a belief, whether through affirmations, visualizations, or focused thought, it begins to take root in your subconscious mind. It becomes an intrinsic part of you, shaping your thoughts, decisions, and ultimately, your reality.

But belief alone is not enough, it must be accompanied by action. Action is the bridge between your dreams and their manifestation.

It's through your work, effort, and application of your strengths that belief takes form. Whether it's making a plan, taking small daily steps, or boldly seizing opportunities, action transforms potential into reality.

Belief Paired with Action is your Superpower.

Together, they form the foundational bricks of creating the life you desire. When you believe in yourself and back that belief with intentional effort, you wield the power to turn your visions into tangible success.

I will share a personal example. I have been up and down the scales my entire life and hovered around 200lbs at 5 foot 2.5 inches for much of it. While I carried it well for the most part, I was not happy at all with what I was seeing in the mirror that day when I woke up and wanted more for myself.

For the previous 3.5 years I had been working from home raising my daughter and managing the marketing firm I created with my ex-husband. After we lost our biggest client, I decided it was time for me to go back to the 9-5 and get myself together. I had delivered at 270lbs and although a good amount of weight had fallen off since then, I was determined to reclaim my inner Diva. My marriage was on its last leg and the lack of attention I had been giving to myself and my needs had taken over my appearance.

Excited to get back to the hustle and bustle of NYC, I took it as an opportunity to reinvent myself. I dove into the Keto diet and kickboxing as soon as I got back to work. The results were immediate, I lost 50 pounds in the first four months. But then the dreaded plateau hit, and for months I made no progress.

What kept me going was my belief in myself. I refused to give up, knowing deep down that I could push past the stall and achieve my goal. That belief led me to adjust my actions. I tweaked my diet, revamped my exercise routine, and sought out new knowledge and strategies to keep progressing. Over the next year, I shed an additional 30 pounds, reclaiming not just my appearance, but my confidence and sense of self-worth.

Belief is powerful because it drives action. It inspires you to persevere, even when the road gets tough. It pushes you to seek solutions, adapt to challenges, and remain committed to your vision. Without belief in yourself, you might stop at the first obstacle. But with it, you can move mountains, or in my case, shed them.

As you get closer to your goals, it is natural for challenges to intensify. The Devil, the Negative Nancys, The Opps, The Haters, or whatever you subscribe to, do not want you to get to that finish line and will do all they can to defeat you. But when you fiercely believe in your destination, these challenges become steppingstones rather than roadblocks.

In reality, you are your own Opp, and belief is your secret weapon to overcome.

Imagine how much more effort you would put into achieving your dreams if you in fact Knew you would achieve them?! Belief is a motivator like no other. It inspires you to work harder, dig deeper, and enjoy the journey. When you believe something, you consider it to be true, and guess what? It becomes true because your belief shapes your actions. Your beliefs determine your reality.

Look around you, every success story begins with someone daring to believe in their vision and taking the necessary steps to bring it to life. Consider Marie Van Brittan Brown, the brilliant Black woman who invented the first closed-circuit TV system, revolutionizing home security. Or Gladys West, another unsung hero, who developed the mathematical code that gave us GPS technology, now indispensable for everything from navigation to weather prediction and military operations. Granville Woods transformed telecommunications with his telegraph innovations, paving the way for Jesse Russell, who pioneered cellular technology, turning our cellphones into an essential part of modern life.

These African American mathematicians, inventors, and engineers (and dozens of others that patented inventions for many of the tools and technologies that every one of us use on a daily basis) reshaped our world because they believed in their potential and took deliberate actions to make their dreams a reality. Their contributions are foundational to the society we live in today, all because they combined vision with effort.

This principle is universal. Every founder, author, musician, or creator also began with a belief in their manifestations. They nurtured that belief, took action, and completed the work necessary to bring their visions to fruition. The formula is simple: *believe and do.*

Here's the truth, you are no different from those who have achieved greatness. The same principles that propelled them forward apply to you. Even if you don't fully believe in yourself right now, start where you are. Pretend if you must, fake it till you make it!! Affirm to yourself every day that you are already what you aspire to be. Belief is the first step, and action is what transforms it into reality. Your greatness is waiting, and it's time to claim it!

Expect Miracles

I've experienced numerous miracles in my life. The first one that stands out was while driving home late from college, I found myself on the verge of swerving into another lane. Suddenly, as if guided by an unseen force, the steering wheel tightened, veering me back in the opposite direction. In that split second, a speeding car zoomed past me, barely missing a collision. It was definitely a moment of divine intervention.

Another instance occurred as I was approaching the end of my unemployment benefits due to one of my repeated layoffs in the technology industry. My family was making preparations for me to move back home into my mother's house, anticipating me not having any income to contribute to the condo I owned with my sister. I instead was calm yet annoyed by their pessimism, and just as I was facing my last unemployment check, a new job offer materialized, seamlessly bridging the gap in my income without interruption. I had a faith that they did not. I knew that Spirit has never forsaken me and always provides for me.

The most magical miracle was in 2005 as I dove headfirst into the creation of my R&B website. Mentally aligned with my dream, I watched it unfold before my very eyes. Week after week, I found myself in the heart of the music industry, rubbing shoulders with legends in record label elevators, and mingling with the hottest artists of the moment at album releases, private parties and studio sessions.

Fueled by excitement and inspiration, I was all in. Nights blurred into days as I stayed up working tirelessly, the sheer passion was bringing my vision to life. Journaling, reciting affirmations, and staying laser-focused on my dream became my daily rituals.

But then, just as I was nearing my launch, disaster struck. The web designer I'd hired to build my site suddenly turned against me, holding it hostage for ransom. He changed the passcodes, locking me out and threatening to withhold access unless I paid him more than our agreed upon fee. For three agonizing days, I felt like the air had been sucked out of my lungs, suffocating in frustration, hurt, and devastation.

On that third day, in the midst of the chaos, I started reciting the bible verse Isaiah 54:17 "No weapon formed against me shall prosper" over and over. With each repetition, I reclaimed a sense of calm and resilience. And then, miraculously, he granted me access without explanation, discussion or even me paying the demanded ransom. I could barely believe it. I was covered in shock, praise and bewilderment as I regained control, locking out the very person who had sought to undermine my dreams.

In that moment, I learned that there is power in calling out to The Divine, and that no one, nothing, no obstacle, no matter how daunting, can stand in the way of what is meant for me.

The Brickhouse Mindset Phase I

My Dear Brickhouse, take control of your mind and enjoy the process of creating the life that you desire. Push past the loud voice in our heads that keep us focused on what is wrong with life, and refocus on the joys and desires of life, knowing that more will come. If you do not give your mind a goal or a plan, you will stay living in the soup of your experiences. Your life will be directed by outside programming, the desires of other people, your fears, and limited expectations.

You risk becoming someone whose life is shaped entirely by chance and circumstance. You settle for dating whoever happens to approach you, regardless of whether they align with your values or goals. You remain stuck in a job you took years ago simply because they offered it, even though it drains your energy, and you've longed to pursue something more fulfilling. Instead of taking action, you find yourself repeatedly complaining about the things you dislike about your life or yourself yet doing little to change them.

In other words, you may not become the person you want to be, you will live a life of limitations rather than achievements. You will be the person who accepts what comes to you rather than the one who creates the life that you want. You will accept the challenges of life as closed doors instead of opening and creating your own doors. Give your mind a plan to experience and watch how it manifests.

Code Switch away from past disappointments and find peace and possibility in the now. Feed your mind with the joy and knowledge that are the bricks that lead to your desired reality. Affirm who you are and what you want every day through your verbal and written words. Believe in your desires and be open to miracles. The more you repeat these actions, the more they become ingrained in your lifestyle, psyche and default programming. The easier and more frequently they will instantly raise your vibration, aligning you with your highest good.

Homework
Objective: Transition from doubt to knowing that your dreams are achievable.

> **Step 1**: Write down one goal you currently desire but feel unsure about achieving.
>
> **Step 2**: Create a vision board or digital collage representing this goal as already achieved.
>
> **Step 3**: Spend 5 minutes each day visualizing your life with this goal fulfilled. Focus on how it feels to live in this reality.
>
> **Reflection**: Journal about moments when you felt aligned with your vision. Did opportunities or ideas arise to support your goal?

- Chapter 6 -

- Chapter 6 -
The Brickhouse Mindset Phase II
Framework for Goal Attainment

Brickhouse Mindset Shift: Even the smallest goals need a plan to know where I am and what's next.

I must start this chapter with a disclaimer. Do not feel pressured to constantly pursue big, life changing goals or to do everything outlined in this owner's manual all at the same time. Goals can be as simple as cooking more healthy meals, beautifying your home, spending more quality time with your children, or incorporating more self-care into your routine. You know what you desire, what is important to you and where you may need some help in transforming different areas of your life, so feel free to utilize the tools within as needed.

If you have dreams and goals that you wish to work on, regardless of their size, the steps outlined here will set you up for success. Life operates in seasons, and not everything is meant to be accomplished all at once. There are times when we must seek peace and recovery, while other seasons call for active engagement. It's vital to honor these cycles and understand that rest is just as important as striving toward your goals.

Embrace the idea that your life journey is not a sprint but a marathon. Small, consistent steps can lead to significant changes over time. So, as you navigate through your goals, big or small, trust the process. Allow yourself the grace to grow at your own pace, knowing that every effort contributes to the beautiful life you are creating.

One huge point I must follow this up with is that **many of us are unhappy, bored or craving more in life simply because we are not achieving.** Goals and dreams provide direction and a sense of purpose. Having something to strive for can lead to greater satisfaction and fulfillment in multiple areas of life.

With that being said, dreams and desires are amazing, but they will not come true just by wishing. To turn those dreams into your real-life story, you need a solid plan, like a roadmap guiding you there. As you approach achieving any goal, you must first Code Switch, Feed, Affirm & Believe, so that you mentally align yourself, and the next phase is to develop a plan or what we call a framework. These two phases together are a Brickhouse's secret weapon for bringing her dreams to life.

Why is a framework so crucial? Imagine trying to build a house without a blueprint. You would end up with a heaping mess. Similarly, without a framework, your dreams might remain vague ideas forever. But a well-structured plan helps you break your dream down into doable steps. Having a framework isn't just about setting goals. It's about getting clear on what you ultimately want, determining how you'll get there, and figuring out what resources and support you'll need along the way. Your framework also keeps you on track. It reminds you why you are working towards your dream and helps you stay focused. When things get tough, and they often do, your plan provides the motivation and direction to keep going.

The steps to mentally develop the *Brickhouse Mindset* detailed in the previous chapter are a way for you to align your thoughts, beliefs, and influences to create an atmosphere of abundance and achievement. Next, we get to the work necessary to bring your dreams to fruition. I do not believe that work needs to be hard, but it must be intentional. You must work with the intention of success, and the following framework aligned with a *Brickhouse Mindset* will get you there faster. So grab your planner, take these steps, personalize them for your goals at hand; and come back to them to tighten up and get back on course when necessary.

Step 1: Assess

Assessing your current situation and clearly defining your goals is a crucial step in the Brickhouse Framework for Success. This assessment phase is the beginning step to create alignment with your thoughts, and actions towards your goals. This sets the stage for the entire process and helps you gain a deep understanding of where you are, where you want to go, and what is standing in your way. This is also where you can create new Code Switching Passion Pics, Feeds, Affirmations & Beliefs that align with the goal you are working on, if you have not already done so.

- ❖ **Where Am I Now?** Start by taking a close look at your current situation. Be honest with yourself about every aspect of your life that relates to your goals. Go back and look at your whys also. For example, in working to shed weight, this means evaluating your weight, health, and fitness levels. Use concrete metrics, like your current weight, body measurements, and overall health status. When building a business, changing careers or going back to school, this involves looking at your current employment, your home life, support system, finances, challenges and responsibilities. This initial step allows you to create a baseline from which you can measure progress.

- ❖ **What Do I Want?** Clearly define your goals. Be clear about what you want to achieve. Make sure your goals are SMART: Specific, Measurable, Achievable, Relevant, and Timebound.

- ❖ **Why Do I Want It?** Reviewing and defining your motivation is essential because your motivation can be a powerful tool to keep you on track, especially during challenging moments.
    - Ask yourself why you want to achieve these goals and what's driving you?
    - How do you want to feel or live your life in 3, 5 or 20 years?
    - Dig deeper, and ask why until there are no more answers, as to why this is important to you.
    - Visualize the end goal. How are you living? What do you look like, who is with you, and most importantly, how do you feel?

- ❖ **What Do I Not Like About My Current Situation?** Identify the pain points or issues you are experiencing in your current state. This could be the discomfort of limited finances or a

dream unfulfilled, being close to your desired weight but not quite there, or anything in life that you would like to improve.
- o Being clear about what you are dissatisfied with will reinforce your determination to change.

Assessment is a vital step that provides clarity and direction. By the end of this assessment, you should have a comprehensive understanding of your goals, the reasons behind them, and the mental fortitude required to achieve them.

Remember that this assessment is not a one-time event. As life progresses and hopefully you move closer towards achieving your dreams, you will need to reassess/refine your goals and actions to adapt to changing circumstances and new insights. Plan to assess where you are and what you need to keep moving forward towards your goals on a quarterly basis.

Step 2: Create a Plan for Success

After you identify what you want and why, you must create your plan to achieve it. Your plan is your roadmap to success. It should outline the specific actions you need to take daily, weekly, and monthly to reach your goals. This will keep you connected to your goals

- ❖ **Outline and Track Your Goals:** A goal without a due date is merely a dream, so it would behoove you to create a "What by When Plan." By setting a clear end date for your goal with

the necessary steps for completion detailed on a calendar/chart, you will create a sense of accountability.
- ❖ Take all of your responsibilities into consideration when establishing due dates. Do not create due dates and expectations that will stress you out, unless you actually have a due date like a semester start date, a contractor deadline, or a wedding dress you must fit into, etc. Also remember that the daily steps that you take towards your goals are the wins and are the actual creation steps towards your goals. Each step in the right direction is a step towards your goal.

High Level What by When Plan Outline

1. Identify and focus on the most important goals or objectives and timeline.
2. Determine the specific actions that will drive progress toward the goals.
3. Keep track of progress on a calendar or chart in a high traffic area for regular viewing. Include what needs to be done on a daily, weekly and monthly basis.
4. Establish regular check-ins to review progress and make adjustments.
5. **Brickhouse Bonus:** Be sure to mentally align with your goals daily by Code Switching, Feeding, Affirming, & Believing in your new goal.

The Brickhouse Mindset Phase II

For example:

Outline for the "What by When" Plan: Buying a Home

1. **Define Your "What"**
   - Clarify your goal: What type of home are you looking to buy? (e.g., single-family, condo, townhouse)
   - Decide on the location: City, neighborhood, or specific area.
   - Identify your budget: Include down payment, monthly mortgage, and additional costs.
2. **Set Your "When"**
   - Choose a realistic timeline for achieving this goal (e.g., 6 months, 1 year, 3 years).
   - Break this timeline into smaller milestones.
3. **Research and Preparation**
   - Assess your financial situation: Review savings, credit score, and debt-to-income ratio.
   - Research the housing market: Learn about trends, prices, and availability in your desired area.
   - Educate yourself on the home-buying process.
4. **Action Steps**
   - Create a savings plan for the down payment and closing costs.
   - Get pre-approved for a mortgage.
   - Hire a realtor and begin house hunting.
   - Schedule home inspections and appraisals.
5. **Track Progress**
   - Set checkpoints to evaluate your progress.
   - Adjust your plan as needed.
6. **Celebrate and Reflect**
   - Close on your home and celebrate your success.

- Reflect on what worked well and what could improve for future goals.

Now here is your plan.

My What by When Plan for Buying a Home

Goal ("What"): I will purchase a 3-bedroom, 2-bathroom single-family home in [City/Neighborhood] within the next 12 months, with a budget of $[amount].

Timeline ("When"): Month 1-3: Preparation Phase

- Assess my financial health: Review credit score, savings, and debt.
- Create a savings plan to reach my down payment goal of $[amount].
- Research mortgage options and get pre-approved by at least two lenders.
- Research desired areas, neighborhoods, and housing markets.

Month 4-8: Exploration Phase

- Hire a reputable real estate agent.
- Begin house hunting, touring 3-5 properties per week.
- Attend open houses and gather insights on market conditions.
- Narrow down the list of potential homes.

Month 9: Decision Phase

- Make an offer on a home that aligns with my budget and criteria.
- Negotiate terms with the seller and finalize the contract.
- Schedule necessary home inspections and appraisals.

Month 10-12: Closing Phase

- Secure final mortgage approval.
- Prepare for closing by reviewing all paperwork and securing homeowner's insurance.
- Close on the home and complete the move-in process.

Actionable Steps:

1. Save $[specific amount] bi-weekly for down payment and emergency home funds.
2. Improve credit score by paying off [specific debt] and keeping credit utilization under 30%.
3. Commit to researching the housing market for 30 minutes daily.
4. Tour at least [specific number] homes each week starting in Month 4.

Checkpoints:

- **3-Month Checkpoint:** Financial health assessed, pre-approval letter obtained, and savings plan on track.

- **6-Month Checkpoint:** Realtor hired and active house hunting underway.
- **9-Month Checkpoint:** Offer made and inspections completed.
- **12-Month Checkpoint:** Keys in hand and move-in complete!

This structured plan ensures clarity and keeps you on track to achieve your goal of buying a home within your desired timeline! Be sure to review and update your plan on a predetermined cadence (daily, weekly, monthly...) You have the authority to write your plan in the best manner to achieve your goal. Utilizing a 'what by when chart' will allow you to work backwards in efforts to set the timeline for your goals.

Also, as you work toward your goals, document your process in a journal. You will learn what works and what does not, identify repeated cycles, lessons and your secret sauce. Be open to refining your plans and strategies based on your successes and failures. Adaptability and the willingness to change your approach are keys to long-term success.

Step 3: Activate

For much simpler goals like maybe you want to incorporate more self-care into your life, or bake more, you can merge Step 2: Create Your Plan for Success & Step 3: Activate.

Schedule your life for Success: As you are mentally aligning with your goals by incorporating your goals into your Passion Pics, media, and affirmations etc., you need to identify where you will incorporate these and the necessary action steps for your specific goals into your daily routine.

My suggestion for the best way to approach this is to set a reminder on your phone every Sunday, entitled "*Schedule your Week*". Then, think about everything that you must and want to get done this week and schedule the time on a written and/or digital calendar. Set reminders on your phone for each action needed.

A process may look like this:

- First, take a thorough assessment of all your responsibilities for the week so that you can put them on a calendar with notifications.
- Be sure to look through your personal and work calendars, your family's schedule and any networking or social activities that you engage in.
- Take note of everything needed to fully complete the task, including any prep or driving time required and set a notification on your phone for the start times.
    - For example, if I need to take BabyGirl to gymnastics at 3:30 on Friday, I set a reminder for 2:30 to "Prep for gymnastics". This allows time for me to gather her gymnastics attire, after school snacks and leave to pick her up from school.

Be as specific as possible to reduce stress and allow room for emergencies and last-minute adjustments. Make sure that you schedule time for your workouts, early morning routine, cooking/meal prep, your children's activities, fun, and rest. Everything should be on a calendar with a notification, especially in the beginning in efforts to get you into the practice of building your lifestyle/routine and sticking to it.

My weekly alerts may include:

- Call 'client' to confirm next steps meeting
- Prep to pick-up child from school (snacks, gymnastics bag, change of clothes)
- Search for IG Reel audio
- Meditation/Visualization
- Book massage for next week
- Put phone on silence for 2 hours of writing
- Eggs, lentils, garbage bags
- Find an editor
- IG Reel recording time

I have tested many calendar apps, and the blue 'RE.minder' app in the iPhone AppStore is free and one of my best tools. This app is a necessity for me because it allows me to set a reminder alert for a task and will set off a notification every minute or every hour, until I check it off as completed. This has tremendously improved the chances of me doing the thing, because if I don't do it, I will get an annoying alert every minute or every hour, and this 9 times out of 10 ensures that my task is completed. I am careful not to delete a reminder that needs to be done, because I can simply extend the reminder to alert me again at a better time if I happen to be tied-up or unable to do the thing at the time I set the reminder for. If I do not set a reminder in my phone, it significantly delays or eliminates the success of me completing the task. Sometimes, just the act of setting the reminder, later reminds me to do the thing because the act of inputting this event in my phone was an experience that caused me to remember.

I promise you, this act alone of taking the time to schedule your week every Sunday will start to help automate your life for success. You will begin to maintain a cycle of focused planning and implementation. You will begin to complete life's necessities and also schedule your alone time, self-care and business development time, all within the same number of hours you did not think could possibly allow room for.

This will start to create a lifestyle that leads you to success in every area of your life. You will identify where you may need to pull your partner in or a baby-sitter in advance, so you can complete your tasks. You will identify the locations/situations that allow you to produce the best work. Your brain will be reprogrammed, and these responsibilities will become easier to manage because you have planned for them.

Step 4: Repeat

The *Brickhouse Mindset* framework will help you build a lifestyle that supports your goals. Keep repeating your plans day after day, month after month. Consistency is the key to turning your goals into reality. Sometimes success is just around the corner, and if you give up too soon, you might miss out on incredible opportunities. No matter how challenging it may seem, remember that you have the capability to make it happen. Activate your plans, and day by day you will get closer to your dreams.

Monitor and Adjust: Regularly review your progress. This step is crucial to ensure that you are staying on track. If you notice any deviations, needs or obstacles, adjust your actions according to your plan and/or update your plan according to the new needs. Life is dynamic, and unexpected challenges and changes often arise. Adaptability is a key trait of successful individuals. Do not be afraid to modify your plan to suit your evolving needs.

Remember, that alignment is ongoing. You are aligning your thoughts, your affirmations, your process, your partners, etc., and adding new of all of it as you grow within your new lifestyle. Whenever you start to get overwhelmed, pause, breathe and activate your Passion Pic. Find peace in the next moment and then readjust your thoughts on your end goals. Take a break if you need to; rest and have some fun, and then come back to your plan refreshed. As you consistently align your actions with your goals and make progress, you will build the momentum and confidence to conquer your distractions and continue to win!

Achieve and keep Achieving: Many people are depressed and feel stuck in life simply because they are not achieving. When you achieve a goal, it makes you feel incredible and eager to achieve more and have more of this good feeling and the things that go along with it. This 'high' affects every aspect of your life. This feeling can catapult you past obstacles and keeps you excited by the journey. It is the journey that is to be savored as you move from achievement to achievement. This creates the joys of life, and one well lived. If you are bored, you are not building your best life.

When you were a child and learned how to walk, then run, tie your shoes, ride a bike, braid your doll's hair, then your own; each of these achievements made it easier for you to reach for and then achieve the next achievement. Each win builds your confidence, knowledge, and ability. This is how a Brickhouse is Built. Win by win, step by step, mindset shift by mindset shift. Believe that you can and deserve the win. Do the work, seek happiness, celebrate yourself and keep building!

As you do this, your accomplishments will increase, people will see you and treat you differently, you will look at and treat yourself differently, better and the cycle continues. How awesome is it to live from a place of love, light, and optimism! This is Bliss. This is the life that the Divine promised you. The land of milk and honey, where you can design your definition of success and bask in its ease. Your definition of success is different from my definition of success, and our definitions will change as we grow. What you wanted in your 20s is different in your 40s.

Your life goals should include a lifestyle and a feeling, not just focused on things.

Of course, the feeling is made better because of nice things, but you are not attached to these things, because they do not make your life. They just add to it and can be replaced.

PART II:

Manifesting A Life That You Love

- Chapter 7 -

Love Yourself

Brickhouse Mindset Shift: The more I love myself, the more I become the woman I desire to be.

Within the *Brickhouse Mindset*, self-love and self-awareness are not just ideals, they are foundational pillars. They work hand in hand to guide you toward living authentically, embracing your worth, and creating a life rooted in peace and purpose. Both are essential for manifesting the life of your desires and navigating challenges with grace and resilience.

> The way you love yourself sets the standard for how others will treat you.

When you value and respect yourself, you communicate to the world that you deserve the same in return. But self-love goes beyond setting boundaries with others, it's about how you treat yourself in the quiet moments when no one else is around. Are you gentle with your thoughts? Do you forgive yourself for mistakes? Do you celebrate your achievements, no matter how small? These are the ways self-love manifests in everyday life.

Without self-love, you risk living a life dictated by external forces, whether it's seeking approval from others, chasing achievements for the sake of worthiness, or staying in relationships that diminish your light. Loving yourself fiercely means choosing to honor your worth, even when it feels difficult or unfamiliar.

Your relationship with yourself is the longest and most significant relationship you'll ever have. It's your responsibility to make it a loving one. You wouldn't neglect a friend who needed support, criticize a loved one for their mistakes, or deny someone rest and nourishment. So why do we so often do these things to ourselves?

> Loving yourself is an act of accountability. It's about recognizing that no one else can give you the care and attention you need as deeply as you can.

When you love yourself, you're not only honoring the Divine energy within you but also giving yourself the strength and stability to show up fully in the world. You cannot pour into others if you are depleted; self-love ensures that your cup is always full.

When you love yourself fiercely, you radiate confidence, peace, and joy, and that energy impacts everyone around you. Your self-love inspires others to love themselves, creating a ripple effect that transforms not only your life but also the lives of those who encounter your light.

Loving yourself also prepares you to receive love. It allows you to recognize when someone's intentions align with your highest good and to walk away from relationships or situations that do not serve you. When you know your worth, you naturally attract people and experiences that affirm it.

Love Yourself

You are not an accident or an afterthought; you are a unique expression of creation, and your presence in this world is significant. When you love yourself, you align with the infinite power that resides within you, giving you the strength to overcome challenges, the wisdom to navigate life, and the courage to pursue your dreams.

Dear Brickhouse, remember this: **loving yourself is not just a one-time decision; it's a daily practice.** It's choosing to show up for yourself every day, even when it's hard. It's forgiving yourself for missteps, celebrating your victories, and nurturing your soul with compassion. When you commit to loving yourself, you create a life of peace, fulfillment, and joy, and that, my dear, is the ultimate manifestation of the *Brickhouse Mindset*.

Without self-love, it becomes challenging to manifest your desires because you may not feel that you deserve them. Without self-love it can become equally challenging to authentically love others or attract genuine love into your life. Without a deep appreciation for your own worth, you may settle for attention rather than true affection, mistaking fleeting gestures for genuine care. Self-love also creates a foundation for healthy relationships, as it allows you to identify when someone is treating you with respect and care, and when they are not.

Self-love is the anchor that keeps you steady in turbulent waters. It's the act of embracing yourself fully, your strengths, your flaws, your victories, and your mistakes. Without self-love, even the strongest mindset can falter. Self-love gives you the courage to set boundaries, to say no to what doesn't serve you, and to pursue the things that bring you joy and fulfillment.

When you love yourself, you stop seeking validation from others and begin to trust your own instincts.

I discovered the true meaning of love when I welcomed my daughter into the world. From that moment on, I devoted myself to her care with unwavering dedication. I ensured she ate the most nutritional foods, bathed her tenderly with the finest products, adorned her in the most comfortable attire, provided her with the safest environments and surrounded her with prayers and affirmations of love and protection. Just as I nurtured my daughter, it became clear that I needed to extend the same level of care to myself.

The initial homework assignments in this book focused on discovering your identity and desires in efforts to develop a love and understanding of yourself, which is essential for personal growth and fulfillment. When you prioritize honoring yourself, you cultivate the love and energy necessary to enhance every aspect of your life.

In the chapters of this book, I outline practices that facilitate self-care and nurture the spirit, vital aspects of loving oneself. These practices encompass how we speak to ourselves, the company we keep, the nourishment we provide our minds, bodies and souls, and the choices we make to honor our own well-being over external expectations.

Love Yourself

> It's about reprogramming our internal dialogue, shifting away from narratives of hurt or lack, and towards embracing our inherent beauty, the beauty of the present moment, and accepting ourselves where we are right now.

This process is an act of self-love, a commitment to nurturing our own needs and aspirations.

By first tending to our own needs and loving ourselves unconditionally, we lay the foundation for personal growth and fulfillment. Let's activate this process by loving yourself enough to identify the sometimes small steps that you can take each day to create a life full of joy, peace and accomplishment.

Create a Life that You Love

> Creating a life that you love is one of the most profound and empowering goals you can set for yourself.

It's a journey toward fulfillment, alignment, and happiness, where each decision, relationship, and experience reflect who you authentically are. Building this life requires clarity, courage, and commitment to your own well-being and growth. It's about making choices that resonate with your heart, values, and aspirations, allowing you to live authentically and fully, and the details within the *Brickhouse Mindset* are designed to activate every facet of creating your best life.

When you live a life aligned with your desires and values, everything flows with greater ease. You experience a sense of purpose and inner peace, and even when challenges arise, you're more resilient because you're living in harmony with yourself. A life you love supports not only your own happiness but also the positive impact you have on those around you. When you're happy, fulfilled, and empowered, your relationships, career, and overall well-being benefit. You become an inspiration to others, showing them what's possible when they prioritize themselves and align with their true purpose.

Take the time to explore what truly matters to you. Reflect on your passions, values, and the experiences that bring you joy. Ask yourself questions like, *what do I love doing? What makes me feel alive? What are the core values that I want to guide my life?* Understanding these aspects will give you a roadmap for making choices that support your happiness and purpose.

Life is dynamic and building a life you love involves continuous self-discovery and adaptation. Your desires, interests, and values will evolve over time, and it's essential to stay open to these changes. Adaptation also involves letting go of what no longer serves you. Be willing to release situations, habits, or relationships that drain your energy or keep you from growing. This creates space for new opportunities and experiences that align with your vision. Embrace change as a natural part of building a life you love and remember that flexibility allows you to explore new possibilities.

Love Yourself

Incorporate More Joy into Your Life

Living a fulfilling life isn't just about achieving goals; it's about enjoying the journey. Incorporating more of what you love into your daily life is uplifting, adding layers of meaning, joy, and inspiration to everything you do. When you make time for the things that make you happy, you're not only honoring yourself but also increasing your energy, creativity, and motivation. This chapter is dedicated to helping you integrate more of those activities, interests, and experiences that bring you joy

To begin, it's important to get clear on what brings you joy. Sometimes, we get so caught up in our responsibilities that we lose touch with the things that make us feel alive. Reflect on the experiences and activities that light you up. What brings you a sense of peace, fun, or excitement? It could be something small, like reading a novel, or something grand, like traveling to new places. Think of the hobbies you once loved the passions you've been curious to explore, and the activities that make you feel most yourself. Visualize how it would feel to make more room in your life for these joys, and let that vision inspire you.

Once you have a clear sense of what you love, it's time to prioritize these activities.

We often fall into the habit of seeing enjoyable things as "extras" we'll get to if there's time, but the truth is, these moments are essential for your well-being. Start by scheduling time for what you love, whether it's five minutes each morning to belt out your favorite song, an hour in the evening to draw, or a whole day on the weekend to garden, window shop or catch up on self-care. Treat these moments with the same respect and commitment as you would any other responsibility in your life. If reading brings you joy, join a book club and set aside time each day to immerse yourself in a book. If dancing makes you feel free, take a dance class and grab your love or bestie to join you.

Incorporating more joy also requires setting boundaries to protect that time. Often, we fill our schedules with obligations that drain us, leaving little room for what really matters. Look at your daily routine and identify where you can create space. This might mean saying no to commitments that don't align with your goals or delegating tasks and responsibilities to free up your time. Remember, it's okay to protect your joy. Doing so not only improves your mood and well-being but also makes you more present and available in other areas of life and for the people that are important to you.

Another powerful way to bring more of what you love into your life is to incorporate it into your existing routines. For example, if you love music, play it while you're cooking or cleaning. I almost always have my favorite songs playing as a background to my day, and schedule time to get up and take a dance break to disrupt the monotony of working from home by releasing some dopamine to keep me going. If nature brings you peace, make it a habit to spend a few minutes outside each day, or better yet, bring your laptop outside and work under the glorious sun. Infusing your regular activities with things you enjoy can turn even mundane tasks into more enjoyable experiences. This approach is particularly helpful if you have a busy schedule, as it allows you to add joy without feeling like you need extra time.

Creating joy in your life also involves being open to new experiences. Often, we think we know exactly what we enjoy, but there may be untapped interests waiting to be explored. **Allow yourself to try new things without the pressure of being perfect at them.** Experiment with activities that spark your curiosity, whether it's painting, learning a language, or trying a new sport. These explorations not only expand your horizons but also add excitement and novelty to your routine, keeping life fresh and dynamic.

As you incorporate more of what you love into your life, remember that it's okay if it doesn't look perfect. Life is about finding balance, and sometimes that balance shifts. Some days, you might spend hours doing what you love, while other days may only allow for a few minutes. The key is consistency and the intention to make joy a priority, and to acknowledge and be grateful for it. Even small moments of joy each day contribute to a life that feels fulfilling.

Reflect regularly on how these changes make you feel. Notice how your energy shifts when you make time for what you love and how it impacts your overall well-being. These moments of reflection can reinforce your commitment to joy, reminding you why it's worth making the effort. When you feel the positive effects of incorporating more joy, you'll naturally want to continue creating space for it. You're also sending a message to yourself that you're worthy of joy and fulfillment.

Life is a precious journey, and you deserve to fill it with experiences that bring you happiness. Make a commitment to prioritize what you love, protect the time to enjoy it, and be open to discovering new sources of joy along the way. In doing so, you'll find yourself living not only a more fulfilling life but one that reflects your unique spirit and purpose.

Embrace the Power of Play
- **Rediscover Playfulness:** Do something purely for fun, like dancing in your living room, painting, or trying a new sport.

- **Spend Time Outdoors:** Nature is an incredible source of joy. Go for walks, have a picnic, or simply sit and soak in the sun.

- **Laugh Often:** Watch a comedy show, call a friend who makes you laugh, or revisit funny moments from your past.

Leverage AI to Build a Career You Love

Society often dictates that we should all follow the same script: go to school, attend college, get a good job, settle down, and build a family. But this cookie-cutter approach to life is far from authentic.

Societal expectations are not universal, they vary dramatically across cultures and change over time.

What we are taught to prioritize in one part of the world may not even be considered important in another. Even within our own lifetime, we've seen dramatic shifts in how society views work and success.

Generations ago, entrepreneurship and skilled trades were the backbone of thriving communities. Over time, the focus shifted to manufacturing jobs, then to corporate careers. Now, we're experiencing a renaissance of entrepreneurship, where individuals are once again pursuing their passions and building lives that align with their true desires. This shift is a reminder that the societal narrative about success is ever evolving and that the most important question isn't "What should I do?" but rather, "What fulfills me and allows me to create the life I truly desire?"

For many, the fear of stepping outside societal norms or pursuing a nontraditional path has been instilled from an early age. We've been discouraged from pursuing creative or unconventional careers and told that entrepreneurship or blue-collar work isn't as valuable as corporate jobs. Yet today, many of these so-called "alternative" careers are proving to be some of the most lucrative and in demand.

This is where artificial intelligence (AI) becomes a game-changer. It is revolutionizing the way we work, learn, and create, offering tools that can support you in building a career that not only sustains you financially but also aligns with your passions and purpose. Do not remain focused on the belief that AI is going to eliminate your job; instead harness its power as a gateway to creativity, innovation, and autonomy, that can enable you to turn your unique talents and dreams into your own profitable ventures.

AI offers you the ability to turn your interests into a career path that aligns with your lifestyle and values.

Imagine pursuing work that not only reflects who you are but also allows you the flexibility and freedom to design each day around what matters to you. With AI, this is possible, and more accessible than ever before. Whether you're an artist, writer, coach, or entrepreneur, AI can help amplify your abilities, reach a wider audience, streamline your processes, and even open doors to new fields you might not have considered.

One of the most exciting ways AI supports building a passion-based career is by giving you the power to reach a global audience with minimal and many times free resources. In the past, starting a business often required significant investments, both in time and money, for market research, advertising, and customer outreach. Now, AI-driven tools allow you to conduct research quickly, understand your target audience deeply, and create content that reaches people all over the world from your laptop. With AI tools for content creation, digital marketing, and social media management, you can share your creations and story in ways that resonate with others and build a loyal following based on your passion.

AI reduces or even eliminates the need for a large team by automating essential tasks, streamlining processes, and performing functions that traditionally required several employees. With AI-powered tools, entrepreneurs can now independently handle key areas of their business, from customer service to marketing to data analysis, allowing them to save on staffing costs without sacrificing efficiency.

Another revolutionary aspect of AI is its capacity for enhancing creativity. If you're a writer, artist, or designer, AI tools can offer fresh ideas, inspiration, and even drafts or mockups that spark your own creative process. AI can generate ideas based on your input, provide suggestions for new content, and even help you visualize concepts. This collaboration between human creativity and AI-driven insights opens new realms of possibility, allowing you to create work that's innovative and uniquely yours. AI doesn't replace your originality; it amplifies it, giving you the confidence and resources to push your creative boundaries.

To make the most of AI as you build a career around your passions, it's essential to approach it as a tool that supports your vision rather than something that defines it. Begin by clarifying what you genuinely enjoy, your strengths, and how you want to make an impact. Then, consider how AI can help you in specific areas, such as content creation, marketing, customer engagement, and administrative tasks. Research and experiment with various AI tools, explore their potential, and find a combination that complements your work style and enhances your ability to create, connect, and grow. Again, many of these tools are free or low cost, and you can find out more about them by scouring the internet or reaching out to your local chamber of commerce and various small business associations.

As you harness the power of AI, remember that its true potential lies in its ability to support and amplify your unique abilities. AI doesn't replace your personal touch, your perspective, or the passion you bring to your work. Instead, it frees you to focus on the aspects of your career that matter most to you, helping you create a life that reflects your true self.

With AI as your ally, you have an incredible opportunity to turn what you love into a meaningful and sustainable source of income. AI can enable you to become the next millionaire solopreneur, and the first solopreneur billionaire is soon to follow. Don't let fear hold you back from embracing this powerful resource or overlook its incredible potential to better your life. AI offers opportunities that can elevate your personal and professional growth, opening doors that once seemed inaccessible. Now is the time to harness its capabilities to create, innovate, and shape the future you desire.

- Chapter 8 -

- Chapter 8 -
Optimizers for Manifesting Your Best Life

Brickhouse Mindset Shift: Everything gets better when I focus on appreciating and loving me.

Appreciate who you are and be grateful for everything that you have and are creating. By embracing this mindset, a Brickhouse attracts optimism and abundance, allowing her to fully experience the joy and fulfillment she desires in life. She radiates this every day and sparks the same in those that also seek joy.

Keeping that in mind, here are some optimizers that when consistently worked into your mindset and lifestyle, will greatly enhance your manifestation process.

Celebrate the Small Wins

The importance of celebrating even the smallest wins on your journey cannot be emphasized enough. No matter how small and especially if it is something that you kept putting off doing, when it is completed, check it off your list and celebrate! These small wins serve as motivators and fuel your belief in your ability to succeed. These are the achievements that you build on to keep you going. They raise your vibration! Life can get overwhelming, and every step you take towards your goals, no matter how minor it may seem, is a victory worth celebrating.

I strive to enjoy non-food-based rewards or indulgences. After a big win or a week where I checked off everything on my To-Do List, I may take a chill day or do something/go someplace I have never gone before. I often take a Saturday morning and find the best things to put a smile on my face for under $20 or $50. Anything that makes me feel good and does not need to be expensive, although expensive gifts and travel are always awesome as well.

Don't get me wrong, you do not need a reason to have fun or treat yourself. Life is to be enjoyed, and fun should be a regular part of it. Sometimes I just rock out on my deck to my favorite songs to feel great in the moment, go roller-skating or dancing. Dancing should definitely be a part of a Brickhouse's routine as it brings joy and can help heal your spirit through sound and movement. Incorporate celebrations and fun with yourself, your friends and life partners to keep your vibrations high and to attract more lightness into your life.

Be Grateful

In the pursuit of manifesting your dream life, embracing gratitude is immensely important in your empowerment journey. Gratitude serves as the fertile soil in which your aspirations take root and flourish. By acknowledging the blessings and opportunities already present, you attract more of them and keep yourself aligned with the vibrations of success and fulfillment. Like attracts like, so the more you are grateful for, the more you will have to be grateful for. If you do not respect or appreciate all that you already have, you are probably out of alignment with what you want and in alignment for more lack of it.

Optimizers for Manifesting Your Best Life

Gratitude serves as a powerful mindset shift that amplifies your intentions. It allows you to acknowledge and celebrate the blessings, no matter how small, fostering a sense of abundance and possibility. When you are grateful, you attract more positivity and opportunities into your life, aligning your energy with the fulfillment of your aspirations. It becomes a grounding force during challenging times, reminding you of your achievements and inner strength.

You can incorporate gratitude into your journaling practice by writing 3 things that you are grateful for every night. This not only amplifies good feelings, but it provides you with a written history of your blessings, shows the universe that you are appreciative of what it has already brought you, and can remind you that things are not so bad after all.

Select an Accountability Partner

An accountability partner can be an important and supportive teammate on your journey toward achieving your personal and/or professional goals. They are someone you trust and respect, with whom you share your aspirations, plans, and progress. This person serves as both a cheerleader and a coach. They keep you focused and motivated by checking in regularly on your goals, offering encouragement, and providing constructive feedback. This is a person who will support you on your journey and that you must check in with to detail what you have done and/or what needs to be done.

For example, this could happen simply with a quick daily or 3 times a week text to say, "Hey Che', I completed my exercise for the day", or "I finished the third chapter of my e-book this week." When I respond and tell you how awesome you are for doing so, that gives you ammunition for greatness. On the contrary, if you haven't checked in with me, I can text you to see how you are, remind you to do the thing, and/or give you encouragement or direction when needed.

Your Accountability Partner must be invested in your goals either by their personal gain like a with a business partner or from someone who loves you and wants to see you win. If your goal is to shed weight, this may be a friend that is also on the same journey. If you are building a business, returning to dating after divorce or continuing your education, this may be a mentor that has done what you are doing and can provide you with support and beneficial encouragement because they have been where you are. They are the person that you call instead of the one who does not deserve you or when you are tempted to finish that pint of ice cream at 10pm.

The Power of the Pause

I cannot stress enough the power of the pause. The pause is profound. It can be a shield, keeping you safe, focused, and sometimes, it can even save your life. Before making important decisions or when faced with fear or challenging situations, I urge you to take a moment to pause and contemplate the next right course of action.

Often, ideas and conflicts arise suddenly, bombarding us with choices. The pause grants us a precious moment to collect ourselves, weigh our options, and hopefully select the best path forward. Many of us can recall instances where impulsive decisions led to unfavorable outcomes, driven by emotions or a lack of information. However, pausing for however long is necessary; it allows us moments to decide the next right action, preventing reactive responses driven by anger or self-sabotage.

By pausing, we can discern the true intentions of others, respect our own value, and perceive danger. Pausing enables us to step back from immediate urges or emotions and assess whether our choices align with our desired goals. In moments of impulse, whether it's reacting to a situation, making a decision, or indulging in a temptation, taking a pause allows us to create space for reflection. This intentional break gives us the opportunity to check in with ourselves, examining our motivations and the potential consequences of our actions.

During this pause, we can ask ourselves critical questions: Is this choice aligned with my long-term goals, or am I simply seeking instant gratification? What are the underlying emotions driving this decision, and do they reflect my true desires? By considering these aspects, we can differentiate between actions that serve our greater aspirations and those that merely satisfy fleeting feelings. This practice not only cultivates mindfulness but also fosters self-awareness, empowering us to make decisions that resonate with our values and desired outcomes. Ultimately, harnessing the power of the pause equips us with the clarity needed to pursue a life that is intentional and fulfilling, rather than one dictated by momentary impulses.

Incorporating pauses into our speech and actions is paramount. Personally, I frequently pause when speaking, particularly in unfamiliar settings, to convey my intentions accurately or safeguard myself. Simply taking a few deep breaths can alleviate stress, refocus the mind, and facilitate sound decision-making.

The key is to cultivate a habit of pausing regularly. With practice, pausing becomes second nature, empowering us to navigate life's complexities with wisdom and clarity. So, pause, breathe, and ask the Divine to guide you toward your highest potential.

Speak your Truth

Speaking your truth is a fundamental aspect of living an authentic and fulfilling Brickhouse life. It involves expressing your thoughts, feelings, and beliefs openly and honestly, without fear of judgment or reprisal. This practice is crucial for several reasons, as it empowers you to reclaim your voice and assert your identity in various aspects of life beyond just relationships.

First and foremost, speaking your truth fosters self-awareness. When you articulate your feelings and beliefs, you engage in a reflective process that helps you understand yourself better. This clarity allows you to identify what you honestly want, need, and value, which can guide your decisions and actions. Self-awareness is the foundation of personal growth; the more you know yourself, the more you can align your life with your true desires.

Moreover, speaking your truth promotes emotional well-being. Bottling up emotions or suppressing your thoughts can lead to stress, anxiety, and even physical health issues. By expressing your truth, you release pent-up feelings, leading to a sense of relief. This emotional honesty can also enhance your mental health, as it reduces the burden of carrying unexpressed thoughts and feelings.

Many times, we hold onto feelings of frustration or disappointment because we're afraid of how someone might react. That tension can build up, leading to misunderstandings and resentment, and least likely the best relationships or situations for you. By expressing yourself, you allow others to see your perspective and, in turn, encourage them to share theirs. It's a two-way street that fosters trust and respect.

Not being honest in a relationship can lead to an avalanche of negative consequences that can harm both the partnership and the individuals involved. When honesty is lacking, trust begins to erode. Trust is the cornerstone of any healthy relationship; without it, feelings of insecurity and doubt can creep in, causing both partners to feel vulnerable and disconnected.

Additionally, dishonesty can create a cycle of resentment. When one person withholds the truth or sugarcoats their feelings, the other may feel deceived or manipulated once the truth comes to light, and it usually does. This can lead to arguments, confusion, and emotional distance, further complicating the relationship dynamic.

Now, I get it, speaking your truth can feel daunting. It's normal to worry about how your words will be received. But remember, your feelings are valid, and you have every right to express them. It's not about starting arguments or being confrontational; it's about having healthy conversations that lead to growth and harmony.

You can't expect people to automatically know how to treat you, sometimes, you have to teach them.

Many individuals are unaware of how their actions or words affect others, and a genuine conversation can often lead to change. Share your feelings openly and honestly. Let them know how their behavior impacts you and pay close attention to their response.

What is your immediate sense or intuition? Does it feel like they are listening, or are they locked in defense or self-serving justification? Their response will tell you everything you need to know. If they love and care about you and the impact of their actions, this moment of vulnerability can foster mutual growth and compassion. Respectful relationships are built on a willingness to listen, adapt, and improve.

However, if you walk away from the conversation feeling dismissed, unheard, or like nothing will change, it's time to reassess the relationship. Staying in an environment of disregard or disrespect can drain your energy and limit your growth. In such cases, choosing to step away and focus on your well-being may be the healthiest decision. Prioritize your peace and remember that personal relationships should uplift and align with your worth not diminish it.

Ultimately, speaking your truth is an act of self-love and empowerment. It requires courage to voice your beliefs and feelings, but the rewards are immeasurable. By embracing your truth, you not only enhance your own life but also contribute positively to the lives of others, encouraging a world where authenticity and consideration thrive. So, take a deep breath, trust your instincts, and let your voice be heard. You deserve to be seen and understood, and the people in your world deserve to know the real you.

When it comes to family, it's important to approach delicate situations with sensitivity, especially given the generational dynamics of respect. Many of our parents grew up in an era where children were expected to be seen and not heard, and their communication style may reflect that upbringing. This can sometimes result in harsh delivery, even if their intentions aren't meant to harm.

In these situations, it's crucial to maintain your respect while also protecting your emotional well-being. Know when certain conversations are likely to lead to conflict, and don't feel obligated to engage in discussions that repeatedly go nowhere. Instead, manage the relationship in a way that honors your feelings and acknowledges that some issues may never find resolution.

> Limiting interactions doesn't mean you love or respect them any less, it means you are setting boundaries to preserve your peace.

By navigating these relationships with consideration and grace, you can maintain a balance between respecting family traditions and prioritizing your mental and emotional health. Sometimes, the best way to honor both yourself and your family is to accept the differences and focus on what can be shared without compromising your well-being.

If you find yourself hesitant to voice your concerns, needs, or desires with someone, here are some steps to help you overcome your fear of voicing your needs:

1. **Reflect on Your Feelings**: Take a moment to identify what you're feeling and what you want to communicate. Clarity is essential.
2. **Write It Down**: Jot down your thoughts to organize your message. This can help you articulate your feelings clearly and effectively.
3. **Practice Aloud**: Say your message out loud, either in front of a mirror or to a trusted friend. This practice helps you become comfortable with your words.
4. **Choose the Right Time**: Initiate the conversation during a calm moment, not in the heat of conflict. This will increase the likelihood of being understood and receiving a positive response.
5. **Challenge Your Fears**: Recognize that we often imagine worst-case scenarios that rarely happen. When you finally voice your concerns, you may discover the other person is more receptive than you anticipated.
6. **Embrace Vulnerability**: Understand that it's okay to be vulnerable. Sharing your feelings can deepen your connections and lead to more fulfilling relationships and experiences.
7. **Expect Positive Outcomes**: By expressing your needs, you clear mental space for peace and invite positive changes into your life. You may find that the results exceed your expectations or confirm when it is time to move on. Either way, this is a positive outcome.

By becoming more comfortable with expressing yourself, you enhance not only your relationships but also your overall sense of well-being. You'll also find it easier to identify who really belongs in your life and who may need to be limited or removed. The more you practice voicing your concerns, you will do it earlier in relationships and prevent yourself from investing in people who will not honor you or your relationship.

I came from that generation where children were to be seen and not heard, and many of us never released that programming that carried us through adulthood. This may have been beneficial when you grew up in a tribe or a community that took care of its own, where you had multiple generations of the family within close proximity, so that you had layers of people that had your best interest at heart; but in this modern society where families are scattered and the main focus is not the health of the family, but money and acquiring things, we must learn to voice our concerns and needs to people so that we can quickly weed out the overflow of people that will come and go in our lives. So that we can protect ourselves from people who only want to take from us and not be a benefit to our lives.

Having a handful of close friends is a major blessing, especially the older we get. Numerous studies show that many of us only have 1-2 people we can depend on, so do not feel bad as your posse diminishes and your dates become fewer and farther between. As you grow and love yourself more and more, you will only be able to tolerate those that share your good energy and wish you well.

> If people respect you, they will treat you with respect initially. If they somehow lose it or do not treat you in a manner that feels good to your spirit, *immediately* address it, and then set up boundaries, if not permanent space between you and them if the disrespect continues.

Your lack of boundaries is you giving into fear. Putting someone else's comfortability above your own. Get in the habit of using your voice to protect yourself, your time, your heart, your energy, and you will be better for it.

BONUS: A High Achieving Brickhouse is Early to Rise

Waking up early, like 4-5am is a common practice among high achievers. Google it. Early mornings provide focused and distraction-free time to work on your priorities. Whether it is working out, writing, or any other goal-related task, you can get a surprising amount of work done in the early morning hours if you are dedicated and allocate this time wisely.

This early morning work is usually a time of less distractions because your partner or children may not be up yet, and you can get more work done without interruption. It can be a struggle in the beginning to get out of bed earlier, but I promise you, the longer you stick with it, the easier it will get, and then you will begin to cherish this peaceful time for yourself. You will start to see how much more important work gets done during this time.

Optimizers for Manifesting Your Best Life

Use this time wisely to set yourself up for success with meditation/prayer and visualization, stretching, exercising, and doing some self-care. Early mornings are also great for research, writing, planning and tedious responsibilities that require focus. I start almost every morning with about 30 minutes of meditation, visualization, prayer and stretching. I then put on my workout gear, exercise, and get to work. If I am up by 5am, I will have 4 hours of dedicated personal work time before I start my official workday at 9am.

Don't worry about not getting enough sleep either, because at nighttime, you will have less of a desire to do things like channel-surf the TV or have late night snacks, because you will tire earlier and will not want to unravel your progress with things that no longer serve you. You will have a more disciplined and focused outlook and will quite quickly marvel at how much more work you actually completed just by getting up earlier.

You can jump right in and set your alarm for 4:30 or gradually push your alarm back 30 minutes until you arrive at a 5am wake time. In the beginning, do not beat yourself up if you do not actually get out of bed at the set time, but do get out of bed early. The more you get out of bed early, the easier it will become to get out of bed early.

Remember, this is your own individual journey, and I am simply making suggestions backed by the direction of brilliant scholars and winners, which can help you achieve your dreams in the most effective ways. You can choose to keep doing things your way, knowing that you can do better. But a Brickhouse knows that she must challenge herself to find new tools and techniques to achieve her goals, and this one will definitely be a game changer.

You Got This Brickhouse!

Life is undeniably packed with an endless list of tasks and responsibilities that often feel non-negotiable. From daily chores to work obligations, we juggle a myriad of duties just to keep things running smoothly. Yet, amidst this whirlwind of activity, it's crucial to remember that clearing mental clutter, prioritizing self-care, and engaging in activities that resonate with your heart are not just optional, they're essential.

Creating a life you love starts with harnessing your innate power to shape your reality. This begins with finding peace and joy within your own mind. When you make a conscious effort to clear mental and emotional clutter, you open up space for clarity, creativity, and a deeper connection to your true desires.

Remember, you deserve a life filled with joy and satisfaction. By committing to these practices, you're not only enhancing your well-being but also paving the way to create the life you've always dreamed of. Embrace the power you hold within and let it guide you toward a future where peace, happiness, and love are not just aspirations but daily realities.

So, step into your power my dear Brickhouse, and know that every effort you make towards finding peace and nurturing yourself is a step towards crafting the life you deserve. You've got this!

- Chapter 9 -
Overcoming Obstacles to Manifest Your Best Life

Brickhouse Mindset Shift: Every obstacle overcome is a catalyst for success

A Brickhouse's journey is illuminated by love and light, yet it's crucial to acknowledge that life comes with its own challenges, and that working towards true growth, becoming better, or accomplishing great things is rarely found without additional challenges or obstacles. Embracing the idea that growth and comfort cannot coexist, is a foundational step in manifesting your best life. Every individual will encounter challenges, setbacks, experience hurt, and possibly even trauma; the key is to not sit in the pain and allow it to deter you.

Don't Let the Obstacles Win

Whether it's waking up early to seize the day, committing to a consistent exercise routine, the challenges that come with building a business or learning how to be honest with yourself and others; growth often involves navigating through discomfort.

This discomfort is not a sign of failure or to stop, but is a natural part of your journey. The reality is that the bigger your ambitions and the more significant your goals, the more resistance you may encounter. Negative forces, obstacles, and setbacks will arise, often from unexpected places or just within your mind. While challenges can slow you down, they offer valuable opportunities for development. Understanding how to navigate and leverage these obstacles can make a significant difference in your journey toward success.

Here are some mindset shits to help you think differently about obstacles and move through them when they arrive.

- **Opportunity for Growth:** Challenges often push you out of your comfort zone, forcing you to develop new skills, adapt to changing circumstances, and find creative solutions. This growth process can strengthen your resilience and enhance your problem-solving abilities.

- **Redefining Goals:** Obstacles can prompt you to reassess your goals and strategies. They may reveal weaknesses in your approach or highlight areas for improvement. By addressing these issues, you can refine your goals and develop a more robust plan for achieving them.

- **Building Resilience:** Overcoming obstacles builds mental and emotional resilience. Each challenge you face and conquer strengthens your ability to handle future difficulties, making you more prepared for the ups and downs of your journey.

- **Innovation and Creativity:** Challenges often require innovative thinking. When conventional methods fail, you may need to explore new strategies or solutions. This creative problem-solving can lead to breakthroughs and novel approaches that set you apart from others.

Overcoming Obstacles

- **Motivation and Determination:** Facing and overcoming obstacles can reignite your passion and determination. The satisfaction of conquering a challenge can boost your confidence and drive, fueling your motivation to continue pursuing your goals.

When challenges arise, it can be easy to feel overwhelmed and want to throw in the towel. But pushing through is where the real growth happens. The win is on the other side of the test. Acknowledge the discomfort, but don't let it stop you. Take a deep breath and remind yourself of what the end goal feels like and why you started. Anyone who has ever achieved anything great has also had to endure trials and conflict, so be mindful of this and keep going. You will be so proud of yourself once you have achieved your goal.

Embrace the idea that progress doesn't have to be perfect; it just has to be made. Sometimes, the hardest part is simply taking that first or next step. Remember, you have the strength and resilience to overcome whatever stands in your way. So, dig deep, trust yourself, and just do it. You have more than enough tools within the *Brickhouse Mindset* to get you going and keep you going.

When you need that next big push, start by counting down from 3.

3,2,1, Let's Go Brickhouse!

Face Your Fears

Fear is what keeps you trapped in the matrix. It keeps you from believing in yourself and pulling from your arsenal of tools within to protect yourself and create the life of your desires. So many of us never act upon our dreams and just accept the life that comes along, not realizing that you are draining the blood out of the next million-dollar business or a peaceful life. You are stuck in the matrix of lack and struggle and fail to look beyond to other options and the ultimate win. This is not a lack of opportunity, but a lack of vision.

Acknowledging and overcoming fear or impostor syndrome is crucial to success, but then just like any other distraction, remember that this too is in your head, and you now know how to push things out of your head and focus on your success. Instead of allowing fear to paralyze you, confront it head-on, recognizing it as a natural part of the journey. Then activate your Passion Pic, put on your HotGirl music and assemble your plan for success.

> Fear is a distraction my dear Brickhouse.
> You can only overcome fear by doing the thing that you were fearful of.

By facing our fears no matter how small, we gain valuable insights into our strengths, weaknesses, and areas for growth. We learn to trust in our abilities and cultivate a sense of self-assurance that empowers us to navigate the next challenge with confidence. You will see that fear in the rearview, laugh at your apprehension and be even more prepared to tackle the next fear. You are no longer an impostor, but a bonafide achiever. Overcome fear by facing it and doing the thing that you fear!

When it comes to relationships, whether they be friendships or even family, research has shown that relationships where there is a fear of expressing your true feelings and needs can be deeply damaging; but you must take the responsibility to voice your truths and go from there.

If you find it hard to voice your discomfort or when someone disrespects you, then this is a fear that can only be overcome by voicing your discomfort to the person making you uncomfortable. It is that simple. Once you do it once, it becomes easier and then you will be empowered to do it the next time and the next until you are comfortable voicing your needs and concerns. This is so empowering and freeing. It can also save you so much time and heartache from accepting things, people, and situations, which had you spoken up for yourself initially, you could have instantly bettered or have removed from your life immediately.

I am not saying be combative and argumentative. That is the opposite extreme of so many women who accept behavior from people in their lives out of fear. Fear they will leave you, fear of being alone, fear of hurting their feelings while not worrying about hurting your own feelings. All of these fears take up space in our minds and hearts and keep us from experiencing freeing, loving and supportive relationships.

Go back to the last chapter and read about how to voice your truth, because this is a fear you must get over in order to create your best life. This is such an important fear to overcome because it will help you in your relationships, careers, and allow you to release so much unnecessary mental baggage.

Do Not Invite Drama

Drama, in all its forms, serves as a barrier to our happiness and well-being. It drains our energy, consumes our time, and distracts us from living the life of a Brickhouse. Whether it manifests as petty gossip, toxic relationships, or unnecessary conflicts, drama has a toxic grip that can derail even the most focused Brickhouse.

One of the primary reasons to avoid drama is its profound impact on our mental and emotional health. Engaging in drama cultivates stress, anxiety, and negativity, taking a toll on our overall well-being. How much time do we waste thinking and talking about the same old distractions and pain over and over again.

Moreover, drama disrupts our relationships and erodes trust and harmony. It fosters a culture of distrust, manipulation, and betrayal, poisoning the bonds we share with others. Instead of fostering meaningful connections, drama breeds animosity, resentment, and division, tearing apart the fabric of our communities and leaving behind a trail of broken relationships.

It consumes valuable time and energy that could be better invested in pursuits that align with your aspirations and values. Rather than moving forward on our path towards Brickhouse status, drama keeps us stagnant, mired in petty conflicts and trivial concerns.

Everyone has their own tolerance for drama and experience of it, but as you start to feel better about yourself and your existence, by acknowledging the peace and enjoyable experiences that start to come into your life, you will have less interest in it. You will start to pay attention to the little annoyances that it brings and be armed with ways to lessen it in your life.

I am not saying do not be a shoulder to cry on, or empathetic to the challenges of other people, but do not allow another person's issues to become your own. Be with them in the space that they need you, share encouragement and loving guidance, but do not become a dumping ground for darkness. Some people love drama and that is their choice, not your responsibility to resolve.

The next time someone comes to you with some drama that you do not want to be involved with, listen, and only offer advice if asked. Again, many people only want to vent their frustrations and are going to move forward how they want too anyway. If you know this friend wants to do better, asks for your advice, or is in a situation that needs intervention, then offer encouragement and suggest right actions. If you know they are on that BS and do not want to do better, ask yourself if answering the phone or hanging out is for your betterment.

> We all need to have fun and let loose sometimes, but we must also take inventory of our character and the true character of those we choose to associate with.

Determine if the relationship is adding to or taking away from your life. Your mind and body will tell you. For people that are distractions, negative influences or not for your betterment, you will want to answer the phone less or feel drained or even pain around them. Remember to always follow your intuition and limit interaction if you are led. Pay attention to the signs and act accordingly. You know down deep who has your best interest at heart and who deserves your energy. If you cannot decide on your own, ask Spirit to show you and do not ignore the answers.

Extreme examples of people like this are called Energy Vampires and will drain you. They need your healing energy, and it is up to you to protect yourself and set up boundaries. The earlier you determine people's true character and pivot accordingly, the better for you.

- Chapter 10 -

Trust Your Intuition & Take Accountability

Brickhouse Mindset Shift: Trusting my intuition and taking accountability for my actions leads to an empowered life.

My Dear Brickhouse, use your intuition to enhance your life by learning to listen to your inner voice and trust the feelings that arise in your mind and body. Your intuition acts as a guiding compass, providing insights that can help you navigate most any situation including relationships, career choices, and your path of personal growth. When faced with decisions or uncertainties, take a moment to pause, breathe, and tune into your feelings, allowing your gut instincts to surface.

For instance, if the behavior of a new romantic interest reminds you of challenging partners from your past, it's essential to acknowledge those feelings rather than dismiss them in favor of excitement or attraction. By doing so, you can avoid potential pitfalls and choose partners who align with your values and desires. Similarly, in your career, if you feel a sense of fulfillment or joy in a particular project, it may signal that you should pursue that path more vigorously.

If you're curious about what intuition really is, think of it as that initial gut feeling or instinct, the first thought that pops into your mind without reason.

It's that inner knowing or sense of understanding that guides you toward what feels right. In contrast, ego often complicates matters by filling your head with justifications, "buts," and "what ifs".

Ego is often rooted in fear and is the voice in your head driven by who you think you are or what you think you deserve. The mental gymnastics between the two can make it harder to discern what your intuition is trying to communicate, but the feminine energy is intuitive and the more you tap into it, the stronger and more reliable your 'first knowing' will become. You will strengthen your ability to hear it more clearly and act more decisively, while becoming attuned to your needs, your desires, and your worth.

Be intentional about tuning into yourself and the subtle signs around you. These signs may manifest as a voice in your head urging you to proceed with caution or physical sensations, like a tightening in your stomach, that signal something isn't quite right. That first, instinctual thought is your intuition at work; the physical discomfort often serves as your body's way of confirming that something feels off. Ask yourself and Spirit what is most aligned with you and your needs. What brings peace instead of complications.

I often overlooked these signals, as they felt normal in the context of my life. It wasn't until I began my healing journey that I realized those childhood stomach aches and the racing heartbeat I experienced whenever my ex-husband called or texted were clear signs of trauma.

Discerning this connection between intuition and bodily sensations has been a pivotal part of my growth. By listening to that inner voice and acknowledging the physical cues my body provided, I learned to navigate relationships and situations with greater clarity and awareness. This journey has empowered me to trust myself more, recognizing that my feelings and instincts are valid guides in making decisions that support my well-being. Embracing and honoring this intuition allows me to foster healthier relationships and create a life that resonates with my true desires.

Accountability: The Key to Your Empowerment

Trusting your intuition and taking accountability for your choices means fully owning your power. Your intuition often nudges you toward the right path, but it's your accountability that ensures you follow through. Think about it: every time you ignore your intuition, allow someone else to steer your life, or make a decision that goes against your better judgment, you are handing over your power. By taking accountability, you reclaim it. You admit where you went wrong, forgive yourself, and/or apologize to others so that you can move forward with a clear conscience.

Life presents us with countless decisions every day. Some are monumental, while others seem insignificant, but each one contributes to the overall quality of your life. When you take responsibility for your actions, choices, and mistakes, you can stop running from them or making situations worse. Life is not about being perfect; it's about being honest with yourself and making corrections when necessary. If you can admit, *I could have handled that better,* you give yourself the chance to learn and adjust. You step into the role of the creator, not the victim.

Regret, embarrassment, and misplaced anger can weigh you down like a heavy anchor, stealing your joy, straining your relationships, and closing doors to opportunities.

These burdens can even take years off your life through the stress and emotional turmoil they create. Yet, the antidote is often simple: the courage to confront a bad decision, take ownership of it, and commit to making better choices moving forward. Accountability is the powerful moment you stand in your truth and declare, "I chose this path, and now I choose to change it."

Taking accountability for where you are in life means acknowledging your role in your successes and your setbacks. It's about looking at your life and asking, *What choices led me here? What can I do differently moving forward?* This level of self-reflection can be uncomfortable, but it is also liberating. It frees you from the cycle of blaming others or external circumstances and puts the power back in your hands.

When you embrace accountability, it's no longer about what happened to you but what you choose to do about it. This shift in perspective empowers you to make intentional decisions that align with the life you desire. Instead of feeling stuck or defeated, you begin to see every challenge as an opportunity for growth and every mistake as a lesson that sharpens your ability to succeed. Taking ownership of your path is not just an act of responsibility; it's an act of self-love. It's a declaration that you are worthy of the effort it takes to build a life you truly want.

When it comes to achieving these goals we are focused on, accountability is the bridge between intention and transformation. It's the thread that ties your dreams to reality. You can dream, plan, and visualize all you want, but without accountability, those dreams remain just that, dreams. Accountability is where intention meets action, and action is the lifeblood of manifestation.

The Law of Attraction, as powerful as it is, cannot function without the energy of the Law of Action.

Visualizing your dreams aligns your vibration, but it's your actions, your doing, that brings them into existence.

Imagine dreaming of owning a thriving business that aligns with your passions and provides the freedom and financial success you desire. The vision is clear: seeing yourself as a confident entrepreneur, leading a successful enterprise. But accountability is in the action, researching your market, building a business plan, showing up daily to refine your craft, and making the necessary sacrifices to grow your venture. Without these efforts, the dream remains an idea. It's through your consistent, intentional actions, taking risks, learning from failures, and staying disciplined, that the vision transforms into reality. Your success is built brick by brick, with every choice you make to keep moving forward.

Accountability is just as crucial in your relationships as it is in your personal growth. It requires you to take an honest look at your role in the dynamics you create with others.

- Are you setting boundaries and communicating your needs?
- Are you holding your partner, friends, and family accountable for how they treat you?
- Are you respecting their boundaries and showing up as your best self?

Taking accountability in relationships is about owning your part in every situation, showing that mutual effort and honesty are non-negotiable in building a lasting, loving relationship with your partner. It keeps you from falling into the exhausting cycle of blame and resentment that can poison even the strongest connection.

Accountability empowers you to face issues head-on instead of silently suffering or waiting for the other person to magically change.

It's about recognizing your role, expressing your needs, and taking the initiative to create a healthier dynamic or to walk away from toxicity. When you step up, you lead by example, and if your partner cannot do the same, it is easy to determine that you are not aligned or equally yoked.

I realized I was in an emotionally dangerous environment early on when my ex-husband spoke to me with such harshness that I often found myself wishing I could just disintegrate into the floor. I desperately pleaded with him for compassion and understanding, yet he was incapable of either. While his behavior was and is undoubtedly hurtful, I don't blame him entirely for what transpired within our relationship because I chose to ignore my intuition and the glaring red flags waving in front of me. Taking responsibility for my choices allows me to release bitterness and stay focused on making better choices moving forward.

I am grateful for the life we built together and the incredible daughter we brought into this world. At the time, I had married my best friend, and together, we achieved some remarkable things. The relationship, for all its challenges, had many moments of meaning and value. Harboring bitterness serves no purpose, it doesn't heal wounds or contribute to my peace. Instead, bitterness only chains me to the past, robbing me of the tranquility I deserve and blinding me to the lessons woven into my experiences. It also makes it harder to open my heart to someone new. Holding onto bitterness would not only hurt me but would also be unfair to the next person who tries to love me.

By taking accountability and letting go of resentment, I have been freed to grow, heal, and forgive myself for staying in the relationship. It's lifted the weight of pain and frustration, giving me the clarity to move forward with a lighter spirit. Forgiveness isn't about excusing or forgetting; it's about taking back my power and making room for peace and happiness in my life.

This is how you turn shit into diamonds. This journey isn't for the weak, so I encourage you to take a good, honest look at the people in your life and the struggles they carry. If you notice darkness in how they handle their challenges and treat others, be prepared for that energy to be aimed at you eventually, if it hasn't already. Do you really want to invite that negativity into your world?

Sometimes, the answer might be yes, especially if you're stubborn and need to learn the hard way how to love, respect and protect yourself. But let those experiences shape you into someone who no longer tolerates that kind of energy. I hope you all can activate those lessons and rise above the darkness instead of being consumed by it. Remember, it's all about finding the strength to vibrate higher, even in the toughest times.

Remember, you are your own first line of defense.

If you don't make the choice to protect yourself, why would anyone else? Accountability is realizing that no one is coming to save you; you must save yourself. I choose not to dwell on past decisions or beat myself up for them, as that only compounds the pain. Instead, I embrace the lessons they offer, honor my own value, and recommit each day to joy, peace, and success. I intentionally surround myself with people who show consistent respect through their actions and words. While perfection isn't a requirement, genuine effort and consideration are.

My Dear Brickhouse, let go of regret and bitterness by embracing ownership of your choices and appreciating the lessons that come from them. Life is a journey filled with experiences designed for your growth, so there's no need to negatively dwell on where you are or what has happened in the past. Depression stems from too much focus on the past, Anxiety is too much focus on the worries of the future. Your power is in the now. Embrace this moment, align with your deepest desires, and honor your journey by making decisions that serve your best interest. Never compromise on what brings you peace, love, and fulfillment.

Homework
Brickhouse Accountability Framework
Objective:
This homework assignment is designed to help you reflect on your actions, identify patterns, and align your behaviors with the life you desire. Through self-reflection and action planning, you will take ownership of your decisions and strengthen your ability to stay accountable to yourself and your goals.

Step 1: Self-Reflection
Take some time to reflect on the following questions. Write your answers in a journal or notebook:

1. **Identify Your Choices**
   Think about a recent situation where you made a decision that didn't align with your goals or values.
   - What was the decision?
   - What were the circumstances or emotions that led to it?
   - How did it impact you or others?

2. **Evaluate Your Role**
   Consider your role in the situation.
   - Did you act impulsively or with intention?
   - Did you ignore your intuition?

- What could you have done differently?

3. **Recognize Patterns**
   Reflect on whether this decision fits into a larger pattern in your life.
   - Are there recurring behaviors, thoughts, or circumstances that lead to similar choices?
   - What do these patterns reveal about your mindset, priorities, or fears?

Step 2: Taking Ownership

Using the insights from your self-reflection, answer these questions to begin taking accountability:

1. **What Can You Control?**
   Identify the aspects of the situation that were within your control.
   - What specific actions or decisions could you have managed differently?
   - How can you take responsibility for the outcome without blaming others?

2. **What Can You Learn?**
   Every situation, no matter how challenging, offers a lesson.
   - What has this experience taught you about yourself?
   - How can you use this lesson to grow and make better decisions in the future?

Step 3: Creating a Plan

Accountability is not just about recognizing past mistakes; it's about taking action to align with your goals. Use the following prompts to create your accountability plan:

1. **Set Clear Intentions**
   - What is one specific goal or value you want to prioritize moving forward?
   - How will you remind yourself of this intention daily?
2. **Define Your Next Steps**
   - What actionable steps will you take this week to align with your intentions?
   - Be specific and realistic. For example, "I will set aside 30 minutes every evening to plan my next day."
3. **Find an Accountability Partner**
   - Who can you trust to help keep you on track?
   - Share your goals and ask for their support, whether through regular check-ins or encouragement.

Step 4: Brickhouse Accountability Statement

Being accountable is so incredibly important that I want you to write a personal accountability statement that captures your commitment to yourself.

For example:
"I take full responsibility for my decisions and actions. I am committed to aligning my choices with my goals, trusting my intuition, and growing from every experience. I hold myself accountable for creating a life that reflects my highest values and aspirations."

PART III:
Your Relationship with Yourself & Others

- Chapter 11 -
Heal Baby!

Brickhouse Mindset Shift: Healing is the act of reclaiming the power that pain once consumed.

It is essential to heal because pain and trauma can cause chronic stress that begins to wear on your mind and body and can create disease. It is also important to heal so that you can improve your relationships and break any patterns that may prevent you from creating healthier relationships, boundaries and ways of coping and moving forward. Heal so that you can release mental stress and be open for the joy and peace to replace it. Heal so that you identify love and respect and not run from it or embrace the opposite.

Just like with romantic relationships and friendships, job challenges, or conflicts in familial relationships, the time needed to process and heal will vary based on factors such as personality, temperament, and past experiences. While some pain may linger for years, it's important to work towards reducing its intensity and impact on your daily life as early as possible.

Handling conflicts with family members requires careful consideration and possibly the implementation of boundaries and/or an intermediary or therapist to find a resolution. Every relationship is not discardable, but neither are your feelings. Regardless, it is important to prioritize your own emotional well-being.

If someone consistently disregards your feelings or fails to support your happiness, it's essential to set boundaries and consider limiting interaction with them.

You can love someone and still limit the amount of time that you spend with them. You can love someone and understand that they cannot become who you want them to be or understand what you want them to understand. This is where you learn to love certain people for who they are in your life and release their power over your feelings. Their ability to remove you from your peace will become less and less.

This entire book is a healing process, but if you are still asking yourself how can I heal from emotional pain, then the first step in healing may be to let out a good cry or two so that you can release those emotions and acknowledge your hurt. Sometimes we act like we are so tough and that we are not feeling pain, but suppressed pain can manifest in many ways like anger, self-destructive practices and a lack of self-worth.

Tears are not just a response to sadness; they are a natural way to release built-up tension and emotional pain. When you cry, your body releases stress hormones and toxins, which can provide a sense of relief. Allowing yourself to cry can be a liberating experience, helping to express feelings that might be difficult to articulate. After a good cry, many people feel lighter and more at peace, as they have released some of their burdens energetically. Never underestimate the power of a good cry in releasing pain and healing.

Heal Baby!

Identifying your pain and taking steps to heal it are important steps in becoming your best self.

Sometimes the anger you feel is not necessarily stemming from the person or situation at hand, but from deeper or past hurt or trauma. Regardless, your goal is to release the pain and by implementing the *Brickhouse Mindset* and some of the practices below, you will be able to process your pain and move forward from it in a healthier way.

Speaking to the Person Who Hurt You

Engaging in a conversation with the person who has hurt you can be an incredibly powerful step in the healing process. Here's why:

1. Reclaim Your Voice

Speaking to someone who has caused you pain allows you to reclaim your voice. It's an opportunity to express how their actions impacted you, articulate your feelings, and assert your needs. This act of voicing your truth is not just about confronting them; it's about taking back your power and acknowledging your own emotions. It can be deeply empowering to communicate directly and honestly, which reinforces your self-worth and helps you regain a sense of control over your own narrative.

2. Gain Closure

Often, unresolved issues linger and cause ongoing emotional distress. Speaking with the person who hurt you can provide a sense of closure. It allows you to address unanswered questions, clear up disagreements, and find resolutions. Even if the conversation doesn't lead to a desired resolution, it can help you come to terms with what happened and facilitate the process of moving on. Everyone is not able to acknowledge their responsibilities in life and this is more about their personal shortcoming and less about how they treated you. Sometimes closure is realizing that this person will never be who you want them to be, and it is up to you to find peace with that.

3. Foster Understanding

Engaging in an open and honest dialogue can foster mutual understanding. It allows both parties to share their perspectives, which can lead to greater empathy and insight. Sometimes, understanding the other person's motivations or circumstances can help you see the situation from a different angle, which can soften your emotional response and pave the way for healing.

4. Release Resentment

Holding onto resentment and anger can be emotionally exhausting. By speaking to the person who hurt you or performing a healing/release ritual you can express these pent-up emotions. Expressing your feelings can be a cleansing experience, allowing you to let go of negative emotions that have been weighing you down. This release can be incredibly freeing and can pave the way for emotional healing and personal growth.

5. Rebuild Relationships

In some cases, addressing the hurt directly can lead to the rebuilding of relationships. By engaging in a constructive conversation, you create space for repair and reconciliation. It can help both parties understand each other better and potentially rebuild trust and connection. Even if the relationship doesn't return to its + state, addressing the hurt can lead to a more respectful and mature interaction moving forward.

6. Practice Forgiveness

Forgiveness is a crucial part of healing, and speaking to the person who hurt you can be a major step towards this process. It allows you to express any lingering hurt and potentially offer forgiveness, which can release you from the grip of past pain. Forgiving someone doesn't mean condoning their actions, but it can be a way to free yourself from ongoing emotional suffering and move forward with a lighter heart.

If you have difficulty speaking to the people who hurt you, go back to Chapter 8 and do the work outlined under 'Speak Your Truth'. This will give you the outline necessary to voice your pain and best reap the rewards from releasing this pain in any form.

Release Rituals

When dealing with emotional pain caused by others, writing letters or creating a video can be powerful release rituals for healing and letting go, especially if you are no longer in contact with the person who hurt you. Before you begin, set the intention to release the pain and find closure. Understand that this letter or video is for your healing, not to seek reconciliation with the other person.

Start by addressing them specifically and expressing your emotions honestly and openly. Allow yourself to feel and acknowledge the pain, anger, sadness, or resentment you've been carrying. Write or speak freely without censoring yourself. Describe how the other person's actions or words affected you. Be specific about the pain they caused and how it has impacted your life, relationships, and well-being. This is your opportunity to release pent-up emotions and confront the hurt. Once you've poured your heart out, take a moment to read over the letter or watch the video. Allow yourself to feel any remaining emotions, then visualize releasing them into the universe. When you're ready, delete the video or ceremoniously burn the letter or tear it into pieces as a symbolic gesture of letting go.

You are forgiving the person for their actions, not necessarily because they deserve it, but because you deserve peace. You realize that you are holding on to the anger and hurt, and this only hurts you, so you must release it. After the release, take care of yourself emotionally and physically. Dance, take a bubble bath, watch your favorite movie, etc. Engage in activities that bring you joy, spend time with supportive loved ones, and practice self-love.

Another way to heal is to think and write about the lessons learned.

- What did you learn about that person and how/if you should move forward with them?
- What did you learn about yourself?
- What did you learn about people, communication, expectations?
- What did you learn about the journey or process of the thing, experience or defeat you endured?
- How can you set yourself up to win or be better equipped to withstand the situation should you find yourself in it again?
- What did you learn about your happiness and how to stay within it or achieve it?
- Are you putting yourself in less than desirable situations? Why?
- How can you see the problems before engaging in them?

Heal Baby!

Do not look at the lesson in anger, but from a position of growth. Every challenge or discomfort brings an opportunity for growth, which is a goal of life. Every day we are growing, and we should be aligning ourselves to grow better in every way. Heal by learning the lessons and be open for the best moving forward.

Self-Care

Healing and self-care are intimately connected because they both prioritize nurturing and restoring one's well-being. Both involve cultivating compassion and acceptance of oneself. By treating herself with love, kindness and sensitivity, a Brickhouse creates a nurturing space for healing to take place, allowing you to release pain and move forward with greater resilience and self-awareness.

There are many ways to heal by developing a self-care practice including:

- Prayer & Meditation
- Affirming the greatness of who you are and what you want
- Visualizing your desired life, achievements and/or partners
- Spending time alone, in silence
- Code Switching your thoughts away from the pain and focusing on the joy/solutions
- Journaling your experiences and the lessons you have learned
- Focusing on and activating your goals and dreams
- Eating well, movement and exercising
- Scheduling your days to do more of what you want and need to get done
- Incorporating daily walks into your schedule

- Engaging in massages, reiki/energy healing, therapy, spa days, facials, yoga...
- Spending time with loved ones
- Listening to uplifting, energetic or your favorite music
- Doing lots of things you enjoy and bring you peace
- Reading & learning about what you enjoy, wish for and are interested in
- Spending time in the sun, in nature
- Walking barefoot on the earth

Another habit that has greatly enhanced my healing journey are my spiritual baths. This is where you add salt (Epsom, Himalayan, or sea) oils, dried flowers, honey, milk and/or crystals to your bath. There are actually many things that you can add to your bath in addition to the salt, so read up on them and add the ingredients that you are drawn to.

The salt is the main ingredient and has many benefits for your body. It aids in muscle relaxation, stress reduction, removes toxins from your body and increases circulation. In addition, spiritually, salt baths have been used for centuries as a way to purify and preserve the body, absorb negative energy and create a barrier against negative energies. They also provide a space for mindfulness, introspection and resetting a peaceful mindset.

I am a water baby, as I was born in the summer and love to swim or be in the water. I utilize my spiritual baths as a time to meditate and visualize with the enhanced effects of the salt and water. We know that water has long been a part of spiritual rituals for rebirth, connection and letting go. I engage in spiritual baths at least 1-2 times a week or more when I am enduring tough times.

Heal Baby!

Whatever you decide to incorporate into your healing process, please understand that like life, healing is a journey. You may not feel completely free, better or healed after one session, but utilize these tools as often as you feel necessary and when you need additional support, release or comfort.

Developing a Spiritual Practice

A spiritual practice fosters forgiveness of others and yourself, by reminding you of the interconnectedness of all beings and the greater meaning behind your experiences. It allows you to surrender control over what you cannot change and trust in a higher power or universal wisdom to guide you. This surrender brings relief, helping you release resistance and open your heart to joy, love, and growth.

In essence, spirituality heals by aligning your mind, body, and soul, offering not just a path out of pain but a journey toward wholeness. It empowers you to move forward with faith and grace, knowing that you have the tools and the support of the universe to create a life filled with peace and fulfillment.

Developing a spiritual practice can be one of the most beneficial things that you can add to your life. It is a collection of the daily steps that you take to develop inner peace, calm and a sense of purpose, and in many ways can enhance your religious practice or replace it. Religion is a set of beliefs and expectations that in many ways has divided and restricted people for centuries.

Developing a spiritual practice connects you directly to God without anyone in between.

In a world often filled with chaos and noise, developing a spiritual practice is an impactful act of self-love and self-care that connects you with The Divine Spirit that creates all things. It's about carving out sacred space and time to connect with your innermost being, nurturing your soul, and honoring your journey. At its core, self-love is about recognizing your worth, embracing your flaws, and treating yourself with kindness and compassion. A spiritual practice offers a sanctuary where you can cultivate these qualities, fostering a deeper knowledge of yourself and your purpose.

A spiritual practice also invites you to cultivate gratitude and appreciation for the beauty and abundance already present in your life, thereby creating more of it. By focusing on the blessings rather than the challenges, you shift your perspective and open yourself up to receiving more love and abundance, deepening your code-switching abilities.

Spirituality is all about growth. Growing within yourself and within your relationship with Spirit. Learning who you are, developing practices to uplift, cleanse and lead you towards finding peace within. Again, you may already be doing many of these things, but once you set your intention to grow spiritually, find God/Spirit and/or find your purpose or peace, this takes things to the next level and can tremendously expand your world.

The following actions can help guide you. Remember, your relationship with your God is personal. *Brickhouse Mindset* is an owner's manual to provide simple directions so you can develop your own journey no matter how deep you choose to go. The first step is to ask Spirit to guide you and lead you to your desires, peace, and bliss. Ask for signs, synchronicities, and confirmations. Ask for the guidance you need to grow closer to Spirit and to your divine path. Make sure that the practices that you embark on sit well within your soul and uplift you, bring peace and help you make better decisions.

As you embark on your journey of self-discovery and spiritual growth, remember to honor your intuition above all else. What may not have felt right in the past could hold the key to your evolution and enlightenment as you continue to evolve. However, this doesn't mean blindly following trends or surrendering your power to others.

In a world where people, religions, and spiritual practices can be manipulated for personal gain, it's essential to approach each decision with discernment and awareness. Avoid following leaders or teachers blindly, and instead, pay attention to their energy and intentions. Anyone can attend a weekend course and become a practitioner, but a true spiritual guide will empower you to connect with The Divine within yourself, rather than seeking allegiance or control. They will not apply pressure.

Before engaging in any spiritual practices or rituals, conduct thorough research and seek recommendations from trusted sources. Be cautious of practitioners who lack the peaceful energy and the necessary expertise to guide you safely. Trust your intuition and ask Spirit to lead you to the right people and experiences that nourish your soul and align you with your highest good.

Ultimately, your relationship with The Divine is a personal journey that doesn't require any person in between you and the highest power.

Trust in your inner knowing, ask for divine guidance, and remain open to the wisdom and support that the universe offers you on your path to spiritual fulfillment.

The following actions can help guide you in creating your own daily spiritual practice:

Self-Reflection and Exploration:
- Begin by reflecting on your beliefs, values, and what spirituality means to you. Consider your upbringing, experiences, and any existing spiritual or religious beliefs you may have.
- Explore different spiritual traditions, philosophies, and practices. Read books, attend workshops, or engage in discussions to expand your knowledge and understanding.

Set Clear Intentions
- Determine why you want to develop a spiritual practice. Is it for personal growth, inner peace, a sense of purpose, or a connection to a higher power? Setting clear intentions will guide your journey.

Choose Your Path
- Decide on the spiritual path or practices that resonate with you. It could be a religious tradition or more of a humanistic approach that focuses on

developing ones' self; practices include meditation, yoga, mindfulness, or a combination of these and more.
- It is essential to choose practices that align with your beliefs and values. There is no one-size-fits-all approach to spirituality.

Commit to Daily Practice
- Consistency is key in developing a spiritual practice. Set aside time each day to engage in your chosen activities.
- Start with a manageable amount of time, and gradually increase it as your practice deepens.

Practice Meditation
- Incorporate meditation or moments of silence into your lifestyle. This practice helps you quiet your mind, become more present, and connect with your inner self. Knowledge and answers come in silence.
- Listen to and download meditation apps or meditations from Pinterest, Spotify and the like to make things easy. You can also participate in guided meditations initially, with a goal of eventually incorporating more silence into your practice. Continue to ask Spirit to guide your journey to your highest good.

Connect with a Community
- Consider taking classes and/or joining a spiritual or religious community or group that shares your beliefs and values. Being part of a supportive community can provide guidance, encouragement, and a sense of belonging.

Study and Learn
- Continuously educate yourself about your chosen spiritual path. Read sacred texts, books by spiritual leaders, or take courses to deepen your knowledge.
- Seek guidance from experienced practitioners or mentors when possible.

Journaling and Reflection
- Keep a spiritual journal to record your thoughts, experiences, and insights during your practice. This can help you track your progress and gain a deeper awareness of your spiritual journey.

Gratitude and Service:
- Cultivate an attitude of gratitude and service. Expressing gratitude for the blessings in your life and helping others can be integral parts of a spiritual practice. Give thanks for everything and help others whenever possible. Remember that being grateful signals to The Almighty that you appreciate what is given and can accept more of what you want.

Your practice, connection and commitment will grow as you devote more time to your journey. Have patience with it and yourself. Most likely, you will not change overnight. This is a life-long journey, and you will learn as you grow. Everyone is not meant to be a monk or a spiritual leader, but everyone can benefit from a spiritual practice. How deep you choose to go is up to you. Follow where you are led and be intentional.

Heal Baby!

Live in Love!

If you want to vibrate high, do everything with loving intention. Society will lead you to believe that leading with love is a weakness, but it is a profound strength. This entire book is dedicated to teaching you how to love yourself by pouring into yourself while focusing on loving thoughts that feed your mind and desires, but I wanted to pause and briefly discuss the importance of living with loving intentions.

Speak and act with love towards yourself, your friends, family, children, pets and strangers.

Numerous studies demonstrate the magnificent power of love when being spoken to humans, plants, and even water. Love is a universal life force that breathes vitality into everything it touches. Yet, many of us build barriers and speak harshly as a defense mechanism, inadvertently inviting more harshness into our lives. It's a simple principle: treat others as you wish to be treated.

Pay attention to how you communicate with others. Notice their reactions. Do they respond with openness and warmth, or do they shutter and become defensive? Consider how you would feel if someone spoke to you the way you speak to others. It's valuable to seek honest feedback from friends, partners, and family during calm moments. Many of us may admit that we project a tough exterior, but it's important to understand how this is perceived by others.

Softening your approach doesn't make you weak or vulnerable to harm; in fact, it can foster greater harmony and compassion in relationships. In a world that can be harsh, it's easy to become hardened towards ourselves and others. However, observe how genuinely happy individuals often maintain their happiness despite life's challenges. Happiness, peace, and joy are energies we can nurture, much like building a protective shield. Love begets love, while toxicity breeds toxicity.

Despite past pain and disappointment, choosing love brings more love into our lives. Toxic relationships dissolve to make way for loving connections, and time spent alone becomes an opportunity to cultivate self-love and adopt nurturing practices. Each time that I separated myself from toxic friends and partners, they were replaced with more loving and giving partners. The speed of this increased as I deepened within my spiritual journey. For nearly a decade of my life, I mainly interacted with one very dear and close friend, and my favorite cousin; but when I moved and aligned with my spiritual purpose, I quickly found a small handful of new friends that I felt safe with.

I recall a tender moment when I first moved to Atlanta, and a stranger's gentle touch on the dance floor moved me to tears. His kindness stirred emotions long buried beneath layers of harsh treatment from narcissistic lovers in my life. It was a powerful reminder of the impact of a gentle touch. In that moment, I realized that I had hardly felt the warmth of affection from a man, but I craved it and deserved it. It took me a long time to receive loving partners because I was surrounded by people who claimed their love but had a hard time showing it.

Brickhouse Mindset isn't about blame; it's a guide for millions of women to reclaim their self-worth, attract and embrace love in all its forms. By choosing love, we draw in loving experiences and partners, reshaping our lives with each act of kindness towards ourselves and others. I am now attracting partners and friends that freely pour into me and voice their affection and appreciation for having me in their lives.

Release bitterness, worry and anger and watch as your world becomes brighter.

As we learn to love ourselves, we teach the world how to treat us, inviting more love and kindness into our lives in return.

- Chapter 12 -

The Brickhouse Body

Brickhouse Mindset Shift: I love and take care of my body, myself because it allows me to be. This is my first responsibility.

A Brickhouse understands the importance of living her best life, which includes taking great care of herself so that she looks and feels her best. Along with maintaining a Brickhouse mind, and soul, maintaining a brickhouse body is one of the most important things a woman can do for herself. Why? Because even simple tweaks to the way you adorn, feed and move your body can have a major impact on your confidence, health and sense of self-worth.

> Your body is the vessel through which you experience your joys, your passions, and all of life itself. By choosing to love and care for it, you honor the incredible gift of simply existing.

When you nourish your body with healthy foods, move it with intention, and rest it with care, you're not just maintaining it; you're celebrating it. A cared-for body supports a clear mind, an uplifted spirit, and the energy needed to manifest your goals and live your dreams. Self-care is not vanity; it's self-respect. To love your body is to embrace the power and potential it holds, allowing you to be fully present, vibrant, and unstoppable.

Accept Yourself First

Before we get to some simple ways you can improve the health of your body and how you package it, you must first accept it.

Stop criticizing yourself for what you don't like or what is not working and appreciate the body that you have. You are alive, so be grateful that you have the power to improve yourself if you so desire. We are our own harshest critics, and this can be very damaging.

Do not be worried about anyone else that may criticize you because this is more a reflection of their internal struggles rather than you. People that love you will help you become better and see yourself in a more beautiful light rather than just point out your flaws. Once you accept your body as it is and thank it for its service, you can release the heavy energy attached to what you don't like and focus your good energy on ways of improving it. This lays the foundation for self-love and personal growth.

To begin this journey of self-acceptance, we must start by reflecting on what we like about ourselves rather than what we don't like, so we can appreciate our unique beauty. This is partly why I asked you to list 50 things that you love about yourself and/or are good at in the beginning of this book, so you can start to appreciate yourself. There is beauty in everyone and most of the people we compare ourselves to do not wake up looking their most fabulous selves, so we must give ourselves grace.

If you look around at the people you encounter on a daily basis, you will see that most people are not beautiful or well dressed; they are average, so there is no reason to criticize and compare yourself against a small percentage of the population. This includes the ones we see on social media, because you are measuring yourself up against hours of preparation to present you with a highlight reel.

The most beautiful people have the same challenges and insecurities as everyone else, and often do not see themselves the same way as those who wish were in their shoes do. Many also pick apart their beauty and sense of self, struggle with their weight, relationships and financial issues, and some also engage in unhealthy practices to maintain what appears beautiful. This is why it is imperative for every woman to first accept themselves and build confidence based on their self-worth, or who we are inside rather than on the external package we present to the world.

This acceptance doesn't mean complacency; rather, it opens the door to setting realistic and loving goals for growth and improvement, if you so choose. When we approach self-improvement from a place of love and acceptance, rather than criticism, we are more likely to engage in healthy habits that nourish our bodies and minds. Whether it's through exercise, balanced nutrition, or self-care, these efforts become acts of self-love rather than punishment for not fitting a certain mold.

Develop Your Personal Style

Instead of focusing solely on what we wish to change, we can celebrate our strengths and find a style that complements our features. Developing a personal sense of style is an empowering journey that goes beyond just clothing and accessories; it's a reflection of your identity and an expression of who you are at your core. When you take the time to explore your personal style, you embark on a path of self-discovery that helps you understand what makes you feel confident, beautiful, and authentic.

Your style should resonate with your personality, making you feel comfortable and self-assured in your skin. It's not merely about following trends; it's about curating a wardrobe that speaks to your individuality, allowing you to showcase your uniqueness. If you haven't found your personal sense of style yet, magazines and Pinterest can be great places to start. Browse through different looks to see what catches your eye and what might suit your figure. You might also consider bringing along a stylish friend when you go shopping. Having someone you trust can make the experience more fun and help you figure out what really works for you.

As you try on different outfits, pay attention to how each one makes you feel. It's not just about looking good; it's about wearing clothes that make you feel comfortable and confident. If you feel self-conscious in what you're wearing, that energy will be felt by other people. By choosing pieces that you love and feel great in, you'll naturally present yourself in a more appealing light. Keep things simple so you are not overwhelmed with options; this is why capsule wardrobes are so appealing. Less is more.

Another option on your journey to develop your personal style can be found at a makeup counter. These spaces act as safe havens for self-expression and discovery, offering you the chance to explore new dimensions of yourself and enhance your natural beauty. Sitting down at a makeup counter can transform how you see yourself in just minutes. Here, you can experiment with a variety of looks, textures, and colors, guided by experts who will help you find shades that complement your skin tone and highlight your unique features. Trying different makeup styles can be an exhilarating experience, allowing you to uncover what truly makes you feel beautiful, whether it's a bold lip, a radiant glow, or a soft, natural look. Remember, less is often more, and sometimes the smallest adjustments can effortlessly accentuate your natural beauty.

Similarly, visiting a hair salon offers a chance for change that extends far beyond just a haircut. A skilled stylist can help you redefine your look, whether you're seeking a dramatic change or a simple refresh. The right hairstyle can frame your face beautifully, enhance your features, and even influence how you carry yourself. This experience can instill a sense of renewal and confidence, providing you with the opportunity to step outside of your comfort zone and embrace new styles that resonate with who you are becoming.

Moreover, the act of taking time for yourself at these beauty counters and salons is a form of self-care. It allows you to pause, reflect, and invest in your well-being, which can significantly boost your self-esteem. As you experiment with your style, you may find that your outward appearance reflects an inner transformation, fostering a deeper sense of self-love and acceptance. Ultimately, these are powerful catalysts for embracing your beauty, enhancing your confidence, and celebrating the incredible Brickhouse that you are.

Improving Your Body

Along with maintaining a Brickhouse mind, and soul, maintaining a Brickhouse Body is one of the most important things a woman can do for herself. Why, because you are your mind, body, and soul; and your body is what you feel every day, present to the world and is your vessel for love and pain. A less than optimal body can affect all facets of your life including your health, lifestyle, opportunities and inner peace.

See, I have been up and down the scales my entire life and hovered around 200 pounds at 5'2 for much of it. While I carried it well for the most part, and defended it to anyone who challenged me, I cannot say that I was ever totally accepting of my weight. I was the "pretty big girl" with a small waist and cute feet, so I was the exception to some; but in all honesty, I still desired to be smaller. To be able to walk into any store and buy clothes off the rack without trying it on, and to secure the love of those that desired me but would never claim me.

After my freshman year in college, I decided that I no longer wanted to look and feel the way I did and went home determined to get rid of my excess weight. That summer, I got a staple in my ear

Che' Lovelight

and a prescription for fen-phen, the "it" weight-loss program of the moment. To be honest, I was not consistent taking the drug, because I am leery of most drugs, but I was able to shed 60 pounds just in time for sophomore year that August. I returned to school a totally different person. My classmates would walk past me and didn't recognize me; it was an eye-opening experience to say the least.

The black student population at my university was small but the Black Student Alliance had a lot of programs in place to keep us connected, so when shit went down, word traveled fast. One of the most disruptive events was when some of the black male athletes developed a list of all the black girls. They rated us from 1-10 based on our looks, bodies and overall desirability. I found out that I was rated an 8, and the only two girls that were rated higher were two of the most arguably attractive girls on campus. My self-esteem shot up; I was so excited to be rated so highly. I was later told that I would have been rated a 10, but I was still too big, and the discussion was that I was a major disappointment because all I had to do was lose a bit more weight and firm up. The nerve!

I share this story for several reasons. Had I not finally decided that I wanted more for myself, I would not have changed my entire existence in just 2 short months. If you were to talk to most people that have shed significant weight, most lost it in less than a year, and saw major improvement within months. After years of fiercely defending my weight and the fact that I did indeed desire to be smaller, I finally decided that I deserved and wanted better for myself. My mindset shifted from defense to desire, and the weight was gone, just like that!

This is the same way I felt when I hit that same point again after the birth of my daughter and returning to work. I had had enough, did not like the person that was staring back at me in the mirror, and I decided it was time for a major life overhaul. I finally decided to shed the weight and the husband, and both were gone. Once you change your mindset from defense of what is not working to the desire of what you want, you will now vibrate at a new frequency and have unimagined power and determination to achieve your dreams. You are your own Opp as I stated before.

Decide what you want, focus on the goal and it is done.

Secondly, you will never be enough for the wrong people, and that's why your journey of self-improvement must be for you, not to win anyone else's approval. True transformation comes when you decide to become your best self because it's what *you* want, not to please or conform to someone else's expectations. Whether it's your body, your style, or your interests, these changes should reflect your desires, not a need for validation. You can't mold yourself into someone else's ideal and expect it to bring lasting love or happiness. Choose growth and improvement for *yourself*, because *you* are worth it.

Since shedding my 80lbs, I definitely look and feel better; but beyond the weight loss, the progression of my exercise journey is sculpting my body in ways I never cared about. My exercise regime started with kickboxing which I loved, and then moved on to weightlifting and strength training. Strength training has shaved off inches and defines muscles I have never seen before. My walk is different, sexier, stronger, and my face is more chiseled, showing off the contours. My ample butt is finally shaping up the way I want it to, because I am focused on building the muscles there.

These are major differences from when I lost those 60 pounds in college. As I look back at pictures of being the same weight now, my body was much softer and undefined then because I did not exercise. When I hear the weights of women whose bodies I hope to have one day soon, I am often shocked because they are within 15-20lbs of mine, but their bodies are more toned. This comes from sculpting by lifting weights. This is the next level beyond weight, it is tone.

Many of us are so focused on being a desired weight, but it is the tone that defines the body. You see this every day. At 135lbs, a woman can be too skinny or athletic. At 200lbs she can be shapeless or a Brickhouse stallion. It is the toning and development of muscle that shrinks fat and defines the body. Most all of the bodies that you desire to have or be with, tone or focus on muscle building, and this can be less exhausting than running and many cardiovascular exercises that can deter you from working out.

In addition, exercise includes walking, rebounding, Pilates, Zumba, dancing and my favorites roller skating and swimming. You can even join a league like soccer, kickball or volleyball. There are so many different types of exercises out there that can be fun and increase your friend circle, so find one and enjoy the many benefits. Shift your mindset from avoiding exercise to one that looks forward to the body, improved health, and new engagement you desire in just a few short months.

The Brickhouse Body

A Brickhouse Body feels great because it is strong, responsive, and desirable. Your body is less tired, moves quicker, walks longer, and carries more. Your internal systems work better, fight disease better, your mind is clearer, you are less stressed. Your digestion moves more efficiently, your brain is sharper, lymph nodes release fluids, you sleep better and wake more refreshed. These are just some of the major health benefits of maintaining your best body.

It is only in recent history where making time to exercise and eat properly is so necessary to maintain a healthy body. For centuries people maintained fit bodies because of their lifestyle. We had to chop the wood and build our own homes, walk to our destinations, and exclusively carry our children. Our entire existence required much more from our bodies, and kept us moving regularly, lifting, and stretching all day.

We didn't have cars or grocery stores, or even stoves or washing machines. We had to hunt, grow and prepare all of our food, now we order it and have it delivered to our doors. The food we ate was higher quality and less if not at all processed, so it did not lead us to pack on weight like much of the Standard American Diet does now. While we appreciate the convenience, we must now adjust how and what we consume to maintain our health.

Even if you are born naturally slim, eventually most of us will get to a point where exercise and adjusting how we eat will become necessary to keep weight off and maintain our health. Unfortunately, this is the reality of the times that we live in, so do not see your weight as a sign of failure, but more as a challenge of modern society, that will benefit you immensely once you decide to better it. Again, working to become your best self first starts with acceptance of where you are and deciding to take steps every day to get to where you want to be.

I am not saying we all need to be slim, I am saying we should put in effort into creating our best bodies and keeping them at optimal performance by how we move it and what we put into it. All of our bodies are different, and we all know if we are at least attempting to make it the best it can be. I am not slim and never have been, so don't come for me. I also know how much better I feel physically and about myself when I am putting in effort into creating my best body.

Finally, having a Brickhouse Body enables you to attract higher quality partners. Two of the most important decisions in your life is who you choose to marry and have children with. Even if you do not want to get married or have children, I am sure most of you can attest to the fact that the quality of your relationships affects much of your life. It is a basic fact that men put their A-game on for the women they desire the most. Point, blank, period. The more desirable you are, allows you access to more of the men that you also desire to choose from. This is basic math and not an insult. If 80% of men find you desirable, then your chances of attracting the mentally and emotionally healthy men that you desire as well, is higher.

Recent years have heavily promoted plastic surgery as a way to quickly achieve desirable bodies, but this can create more problems for those that do not already have a strong sense of their self-worth. Let's clarify the distinction between a Brickhouse and what I like to call a "BadBody." A BadBody may appear to be a Brickhouse on the outside, but she hasn't done the inner work necessary to enjoy the full benefits that a confident, peaceful soul can experience.

The Brickhouse Body

A Brickhouse aspires to be a walking testament to the greatness of womanhood, someone who is admired not just for her looks, but also for her intellect, spirit and emotional balance. Her goal is to ensure that every element of her life contributes to her overall well-being and the enrichment of her Brickhouse existence. Embracing this mindset means recognizing that true beauty is a reflection of inner peace, strength, and self-love, all harmoniously aligned to create a fulfilling and empowered life.

Focusing on becoming a Brickhouse allows you the benefits of learning who you are, engaging in activities that help you become the balanced and whole soul that you desire to be, and only engage with partners that vibrate with and keep you in the vibration of your desires.

My mission is to transform BadBodies into authentic Brickhouses! While social media often blurs the lines between the two, there's a significant difference. A sexy body might turn heads and draw attention, but without the mental and spiritual foundation of a true Brickhouse, it can attract even more situations and men that may lead to heartbreak and disappointment. A BadBody often navigates a sea of admirers who are drawn to her physically, but without the strength of self-awareness, confidence, and alignment, she risks being negatively affected by these encounters.

Imagine having not only the body to attract the men you desire but also the self-confidence, inner strength, and wisdom to only choose high-value partners who genuinely enrich your life. Now *that* is winning! High-quality men are drawn to women who radiate vibrance and beauty, both mentally and spiritually. Being arm candy might catch attention, but it fades and is easily replaced. By pouring into yourself, investing in your appearance, mindset, and overall lifestyle, you position yourself to attract and sustain a fulfilling relationship with a man who values and supports you. Together, you can create a mutually uplifting and deeply rewarding partnership.

How a Brickhouse Eats

If you're serious about shedding weight or developing an eating plan that optimizes your health, the first step is to understand your body's unique needs. A full nutritional profile, which can be obtained from a doctor, nutritionist, or reputable online services, provides detailed insights into the types of foods, nutrients, and minerals your body thrives on, as well as any deficiencies or intolerances.

This personalized approach ensures that you're feeding your body exactly what it needs for optimal function and well-being. While obtaining such a profile is highly effective, it can be costly and may not be necessary, because there are many, many ways to shed weight or eat in a way that is most beneficial for your body, without specialized testing.

I am not a nutritionist, but if you just want a simple way to eat, I would stay focused on lots of vegetables and a higher protein/lower carb eating plan, cycled with fasting, intermittent fasting, and detoxes. Eat and cook with healthy fats. I use avocado oil for just about everything and do not cook with olive oil because it turns rancid at high temperatures. Of course, organic anything is best, but focus on "the dirty 12", spring water and eat your carbs earlier in the day with a dose of vinegar.

Again, there are countless ways to shed weight, but the key to long-term success lies in choosing a program you believe you can commit to. We are all unique individuals with different needs and paths to our highest good. While there are recommended lifestyle approaches, they should always be adapted to suit your specific circumstances and preferences. In addition, as we age, our bodily needs change, so what worked in your 20s may not work in your 40s. Be mindful of this and seek suggestions for your particular stage of life and body composition.

The trouble comes when we assume there's a one-size-fits-all solution, because there rarely is. Instead, I encourage you to design a lifestyle that aligns with *you*.

> Tailor your eating habits, relationships, knowledge pursuits, and spiritual practices to fit your own journey and goals. The most important thing is to live intentionally, act with purpose, and have unwavering belief in the results you want to achieve.

I am not a doctor, but if you're looking to lose a significant amount of weight, such as 50 pounds or more, I personally recommend considering the ketogenic (keto) diet. It's a scientifically backed approach with decades of research supporting its effectiveness, dating as far back as the 1960s. I followed this method and successfully lost over 50 pounds in just four months.

That said, the keto diet requires serious commitment. It's not a plan you can dabble in or cheat on without consequences. Even one cookie can disrupt your progress and stall weight loss for days if not weeks. To succeed, you'll need focus, discipline, and the mental stamina to stay fully dedicated. While it's undoubtedly challenging, it is incredibly effective, particularly for those who want to lose a lot of weight quickly. I do not recommend it as a lifelong eating plan as our bodies do need healthy carbs for regulation and especially for women as we age.

Brickhouse Eating Tips

Here are a few eating tips that will benefit anyone:

- Cook with natural alternatives to the foods that you like but you know are not the best for you.
    For example:
    - Substitute cauliflower for rice, potatoes or noodles
    - Substitute bulgar wheat for rice, oats or flours
    - Substitute beans, lentils, nuts and mushrooms for meat

    You can scour the internet for creative recipes, and this is a wonderful way to increase your veggies and fiber.
- Roast your veggies. You will eat more vegetables if you like how they taste. That pretty much goes for anything. One of the best tasting ways to eat vegetables is to cut them up in cubes, toss them generously with seasonings and oils and roast them in your oven. I promise you that you will never have enough leftovers.
- Slightly season your oils in the pan, especially when cooking vegetables. A key in cooking is to layer the flavors, so by adding a little bit of the same seasonings that you are putting on your vegetables or meats, you are infusing the oil with

flavor and thereby deepening the richness of the flavors in the meal. The trick is to have all of your veggies/food prepared and ready to go. If you put the seasonings in the oil too far in advance of the food, the seasoned oil will most likely burn, and you will have to start again.

- Meal prep on Sundays so that eating healthier is effortless during the week.
- Use healthy dips/drizzles to increase your vegetable and fruit intake. You can make high protein dips out of whatever seasonings you like and dairy/non-dairy yogurt, cottage cheese, cream cheese or nuts.
- If you really want to be a boss, buy one of those divided party trays with a cover on it. On your Sunday prep day, cut up your vegetables and fruits for the week, make your dips and fill the divided tray. This will make it so much easier for you and your family to satisfy your snack cravings with good things. We already discussed how important it is to prep and schedule for your week, so this snack/veggie prep will be so rewarding. Your healthy snacks will be just as easy to reach as your bad ones.
- Drink lemon, ginger, and raw honey (if you Need a sweetener) often. Add these things and green tea to your diet for many reasons.
- Designate 1 or more days a week to eat meat free.
- Only eat when hungry and/or eat 2 meals a day if you are able.
- Limit or eliminate snacking.
- Add electrolytes or key lime to your water.
- Eat soups for 1 or 2 meals a day, especially in the cooler months.
- Find 3-5 healthy meals that you like for breakfast, lunch and dinner and rotate them. This makes your eating plan easier and less of a 'diet'.

- Incorporate fasting into your week, or on a monthly or quarterly basis to start. You can fast all day and/or intermittently fast. Fasting has numerous benefits including aiding the body in metabolism, digestion and the reduction of inflammation. It can also help clear mental fog and increase focus, all by allowing the body to rest and reset. Research water fasting and dry fasting.

Remember, I am not a doctor or a nutritionist and am not responsible for nor guaranteeing your results. These are just some of my suggestions that may or may not be what you are used to seeing.

- Chapter 13 -
Brickhouse Relationships

Brickhouse Mindset Shift: Only those who appreciate my Divine energy are allowed access to it.

As you embody the principles of the *Brickhouse Mindset*, you'll find yourself attracting more partners who resonate with your values and aspirations. You'll learn to identify relationships that nurture your soul and let go of those that drain your energy. This process allows you to cultivate romantic connections with individuals who celebrate your individuality and support your growth, creating a powerful bond built on mutual respect and admiration.

In this chapter, we will explore practical strategies for applying the *Brickhouse Mindset* to your romantic relationships and identify the characteristics of a quality partner. We'll delve into the importance of establishing clear boundaries that promote healthy dynamics, the significance of mutual respect and understanding, and the ways in which you can engage with your partner to foster intimacy and collaboration. By embracing this mindset, you're not just enhancing your own love life; you're contributing to a cycle of positivity and empowerment that elevates both you and your partner.

Che' Lovelight

Nice vs Kind

Distinguishing the difference between being nice and being kind is essential for a Brickhouse who wants to navigate relationships with authenticity and strength. While both qualities are admirable, they come from different places and serve distinct purposes.

> Being nice often involves pleasing others and maintaining a façade of harmony, sometimes at the expense of our own feelings or boundaries.

It's about putting on a smile and going along with what others want, even if it doesn't align with our true selves. This can lead to feelings of resentment and frustration, as we might prioritize others' comfort over our own needs.

On the other hand, being kind is rooted in genuine compassion and respect, both for ourselves and others. Kindness doesn't shy away from honesty; it encourages us to speak our truth while still considering the feelings of those around us. A kind person acknowledges their own needs and boundaries, which ultimately fosters healthier relationships. When you are kind, you empower yourself and others to be authentic, creating a space where everyone can express their true selves without fear of judgment.

For a Brickhouse, recognizing these differences is crucial for self-protection and personal growth. When you encounter situations where being nice would mean compromising your values or ignoring your feelings, it's a signal to pause and assess.

> Ask yourself if you're being nice just to avoid conflict. By choosing kindness instead, you honor your own needs while still being considerate of others.

Learning to differentiate between being nice and being kind empowers you to set healthy boundaries. It allows you to say no when necessary, to stand up for yourself, and to prioritize your well-being. As a Brickhouse, you embody strength and authenticity, and by practicing kindness over niceness, you pave the way for deeper, more meaningful connections that reflect your true self. Remember, being kind doesn't mean you have to please everyone; it means you respect yourself enough to choose the right path for your own happiness and peace.

In the realm of romantic relationships, it is crucial to understand the difference between being nice and being kind, as this knowledge empowers you to protect your heart while fostering genuine connections.

> Being nice can sometimes lead women to overlook or tolerate unhealthy dynamics, which can ultimately keep you in emotionally or physically dangerous situations.

Here are some examples to pay attention to:

1. **Ignoring Red Flags**: A partner might display controlling behavior, jealousy, or disrespectful remarks. Being nice can lead one to rationalize or dismiss these red flags instead of addressing them directly. This avoidance can normalize abusive behavior over time.
2. **Staying Silent During Conflicts**: In an effort to maintain peace or avoid confrontation, you may refrain from expressing your true feelings during disagreements. This can lead to unresolved issues, resentment, and increased tension, potentially escalating into emotional abuse or explosive conflicts.
3. **Accepting Disrespect**: If your partner consistently belittles or criticizes you, being nice may cause you to tolerate this behavior instead of standing up for yourself. This acceptance can erode self-esteem and contribute to a toxic relationship dynamic.
4. **Overcommitting to a Partner's Needs**: Being overly accommodating to a partner's demands, even at the expense of your personal boundaries, can lead to an imbalance in the relationship. This can result in you feeling trapped or manipulated, especially if your needs are consistently ignored.
5. **Rationalizing Emotional Abuse**: Some individuals may be subjected to emotional manipulation, gaslighting, or verbal abuse. You might convince yourself that your partner is just having a bad day or that you should be understanding, thereby allowing the abuse to continue.
6. **Avoiding Necessary Breakups**: Nice girls may feel guilty about ending a relationship, even if it's unhealthy. You might stay in a relationship out of a sense of obligation or fear of

hurting the other person, leading to prolonged emotional turmoil.
7. **Fear of Losing the Relationship**: You may feel that being assertive or honest about your feelings could jeopardize the relationship. This fear can prevent you from addressing significant issues, resulting in a toxic environment where emotional or physical danger can thrive.
8. **Ignoring Physical Safety**: In cases where a partner exhibits aggressive or threatening behavior, being nice may lead you to downplay the seriousness of the situation. You may choose to stay in the relationship, hoping that your kindness will change your partner's behavior, rather than recognizing the need for safety.

Recognizing the difference between being nice and being healthy in a relationship is crucial. A Brickhouse knows the importance of communicating her needs and prioritizing personal safety and well-being over the desire to be agreeable or accommodating. None of the situations described above are acceptable, and the longer you remain in them, the more detrimental they become, especially if children are involved. Tolerating disrespect can erode your happiness, peace, and ultimately your well-being.

If you notice these patterns emerging, it's crucial to take immediate action by voicing your discomfort and being ready to walk away and focus on nurturing your self-love.

When you 've learned to love and value yourself, you'll recognize that none of these behaviors equate to real love. With this perception, walking away from unhealthy situations becomes much easier. Prioritize your own well-being and choose to surround yourself with relationships that uplift and empower you, rather than ones that diminish your spirit. By doing so, you not only protect yourself but also model healthy boundaries for any children in your life, teaching them the importance of self-respect and genuine love.

Setting Boundaries

Armed with internalizing the difference between being nice and being kind, a Brickhouse can effectively set up boundaries that protect her well-being and foster healthier relationships.

> First and foremost, it's essential for a Brickhouse to honor her own worth. When you value yourself, you understand that your time, energy, and emotions are precious.

Are there certain behaviors from friends, family, or partners that leave you feeling drained or disrespected? Take note of these triggers and use them as a guide for creating your boundaries. This self-awareness empowers you to communicate your boundaries clearly and confidently.

As a Brickhouse, it's important to establish clear boundaries that reflect your values and expectations. This not only helps you communicate your needs effectively but also creates a safe space for your partner to do the same. When you express your boundaries, you are essentially laying the groundwork for a healthy relationship where both partners feel valued and understood. In every relationship you will have arguments, challenges and things that you may not agree on, but there are ways to do so and still maintain mutual respect.

Start by identifying what matters most to you in a relationship. Do you need time for yourself to recharge? Are there behaviors or situations that make you uncomfortable? Once you have clarity on your boundaries, communicate them openly with your partner.

> Use "I" statements to express your feelings and needs without placing blame.
> For example, you might say,
> "I feel …. when you…" **or**
> "I need… when… happens."

If something from your past affects your current relationship, you can say, "I have been hurt before in relationships, so I need reassurance that we're on the same page about our commitment."

After voicing your boundaries, encourage your partner to share their thoughts and feelings. You can say something like, "I want to hear your perspective too. How do you feel about what I've shared?" A Brickhouse knows that boundaries are a vital part of self-care and that they help cultivate healthy relationships that align with her true self.

You can go back to Chapter 8 and read about how to speak your truth for additional support in voicing your boundaries. The most important thing is to approach the conversation when things are calm and for you to be clear about what is challenging or upsetting you, and your desire to come to a resolution.

As you navigate your romantic relationships, keep in mind that your boundaries are not fixed, they can evolve as you grow and learn more about yourself and your partner. Being adaptable while staying true to your core values is a key aspect of the *Brickhouse Mindset*. By embracing this approach, you cultivate relationships that are not only fulfilling but also supportive, allowing both you and your partner to thrive together. Ultimately, setting boundaries is an empowering act of self-love that paves the way for healthier, more meaningful romantic connections.

Additionally, remember that enforcing boundaries may feel uncomfortable at first, especially if you're used to being nice at the expense of your own needs. It's okay to feel a little anxious about it. However, practicing kindness both toward yourself and others makes the process easier. Approach boundary-setting as a dialogue rather than a confrontation.

Lastly, be prepared for a range of reactions when you start setting boundaries. Some people may respond positively, appreciating your honesty and clarity. A healthy partner will appreciate your honesty and willingness to communicate. They may even feel inspired to share their own boundaries, leading to deeper compassion and intimacy between you. Others may be taken aback, especially if they're used to you being overly accommodating. Stand firm in your choices, reminding yourself that you deserve to live in alignment with peace and your truth.

> You must also understand when someone is unwilling to change or to be sensitive to your needs and wellbeing.
> If you keep having the same conversations with someone who changes for a short period and reverts to hurtful behaviors, sooner than later you must activate your boundary and exit the relationship.

It's obviously not getting better. There is someone out there that is willing to partner with you in a healthy way. There is no reason to tolerate repeated pain from someone who is supposed to love you.

Dating Basics

> A Brickhouse knows that it's essential for a woman to only allow herself to be courted by a proper mate.

Traditionally, it's been the man's responsibility to demonstrate his value and commitment to the woman he desires. Throughout history, many cultures have respected this by requiring a man to prove himself worthy in the eyes of a woman's family and to pay a dowry before marrying her. This practice underscores the value a woman brings not only to her husband but also to her family.

Despite what social media might suggest, the most successful and desirable men understand and deeply value the significance of a healthy relationship with a good woman. Studies have consistently shown that men in committed relationships often experience greater stability, higher incomes, and better health outcomes, factors frequently attributed to the support and encouragement of their partners.

Brickhouses, remember this as you navigate the dating world: a quality man recognizes the value of a quality woman beyond surface-level attributes. He sees her as a source of strength, inspiration, and partnership. Your love, support, and wisdom are assets for any man. Choose to only align yourself with partners who appreciate your worth and leave the rest alone.

You'll know a man wants you when you don't have to beg for his affection.

A man demonstrates his interest through his actions, just like we do. It's important to note that while he may not always be overtly affectionate, it doesn't mean he doesn't care deeply for you. Men often express their feelings in different ways. For example, he might prioritize quality time with you, support your goals, or show his commitment by being reliable and providing for you. In addition, men often know very early on if you are someone that he can settle down with. If so, his affection will let you know. If he is unsure, take your time and do not make him a priority until he makes you one.

A Brickhouse knows that if a man isn't showing affection, it may simply mean he's not the right fit for her. This realization doesn't make her question her worth, beauty, or desirability. She understands that not everyone is meant for her, just as she isn't meant for everyone. We've all witnessed enough public relationships to know that even the most desirable people can face rejection, betrayal, and disrespect. Embracing this truth empowers a Brickhouse to focus on those who truly appreciate and value her for who she is.

She doesn't need to harbor any animosity toward this man either, because his rejection serves as her protection. It shields her from getting involved with someone who doesn't desire her or who might not be emotionally, mentally, or financially ready to date. Remember, just because someone isn't pursuing you properly doesn't mean they're a bad person. It's impossible for everyone we desire to want us back, life simply doesn't work that way. If that were the case, we would lose the ability to appreciate and value what we have.

I understand you might spend a lot of time thinking about your crush and wishing he would come around. But the sooner you acknowledge that if he really wanted to be with you, he would, the sooner you can free up space in your heart and mind for people and things that instead bring you joy. It's like seeing a beautiful dress in a store that you didn't buy. You might think about it for a few days, but eventually, you move on, and your attachment begins to fade. Even if you had bought that dress, if it didn't fit well or didn't look great on you, you probably wouldn't wear it often.

The simplest way to approach dating is to embrace the people who genuinely make you feel good and appreciated.

This should be your primary focus if you want to be happy. When we chase after or lust for individuals who don't reciprocate our feelings, we only invite pain, disrespect, and sadness into our lives. Instead, love those who love you back, and you'll find that your life becomes much more fulfilling.

Rather than clinging desperately to someone who doesn't treat you the way you want to be treated, stalking their social media or pressuring them for more, a Brickhouse knows when to let go. She understands that if a man is showing her through his actions that she isn't a priority, it's time to remove him from her life. For her, being in a loving relationship is a blessing that should be earned, not taken for granted.

A Brickhouse invests time and effort into herself and her desires, so anyone who isn't willing to put in the same effort to build a meaningful relationship with her simply doesn't deserve to be in her life. She carries herself with confidence, knowing that if a man isn't stepping up, that's perfectly okay. There are plenty of men out there who will appreciate her for who she is. In the meantime, she's busy creating her best life. By living authentically and vibrating at her highest frequency, she will attract a man who is also living his best life, and in due time, their paths will cross.

Many of us get so caught up in the quest for "the one" that we often overlook the quality and value of our partners. Acting as if the goal is simply to be in a relationship, regardless of whether that person feels good for our hearts and spirits. Do you enjoy being with this person? Are the benefits they bring to your life worth the pain or instability they may also bring? Why do we even entertain relationships that cause us more hurt than happiness? While it's true that life can be painful at times, we often accept more pain than necessary in our pursuit of love. In doing so, we compromise our own well-being, subjecting ourselves to individuals who repeatedly hurt our hearts and feelings.

The first time someone starts putting you down, talks to you disrespectfully, or hurts you in any way, this is a serious red flag. You must address it and put a fear in them that you are gone the next time.

Most importantly, you must follow through with that promise. I am not saying that it is absolutely necessary to completely sever ties with every man that disrespects you, but you must remove yourself and/or implement consequences in order to determine if they deserve a chance to redeem themselves. That being said no body deserves repeated chances and physical assault and/or emotional abuse are indeed grounds for you to immediately exit a relationship permanently.

People may test you to see how much of their nonsense you will tolerate, so once they get away with it once, they know they can continue to have their way with you. This is why you cannot just let the situation go just so you can keep the peace or out of fear of conflict or confrontation. The peace has already been disrupted. The conflict has already happened. If you ignore it, that is a signal that the behavior has no consequences. Once you voice your displeasure and it continues, that is confirmation that this is how this person chooses to operate with you, and it is up to you to protect yourself and leave.

People usually show us their best representative in the beginning of a relationship, so once someone disrespects you, especially early in the relationship, you can only expect that disrespect or abuse to continue and get worse. Think about the people you love, cherish or respect in your life. Would you ever treat them in a way that diminishes them? So why would you allow someone to continue to hurt you?

Being alone is better than being battered physically or mentally. Mental abuse is often harder to identify than physical abuse, so this is why paying attention to your intuition or your first thought or knowing is important. Someone that loves you is not playing mind games, making you the villain while hurting your feelings, nor constantly making you feel less than respected, loved or safe.

A person who desires or loves you will find a way to communicate with you in a way that doesn't break you down.

This is your life and future, and you must value yourself and only entertain people that value you as well.

Feminine energy is intuitive, creative, emotional, nurturing, and receptive, while masculine energy is characterized by action, logic, focus, and stability. Both energies are essential, both within us and in our relationships. Problems arise when there's an imbalance. A genuine connection, mutual respect, and a commitment to shared goals are vital. If you look at successful, high-achieving men, most of them are married, and peace is the number one characteristic men require when selecting a wife. You should embrace this need too.

So, if you find yourself in a relationship with a man who doesn't provide a sense of peace and security, then you must ask yourself why you are in this relationship. Sure, the initial allure of the drama and excitement that comes with the bad-boys can be fun, but it's crucial to reflect on how this person contributes to your life and overall well-being. Consider whether they enhance your happiness or just add to your stress. It's necessary to prioritize your peace and embrace relationships that uplift you rather than weigh you down.

> Staying in a relationship that you have to fight to maintain is robbing you of a relationship with someone that actually desires you.

Be Patient and Aware

Another thing to keep in mind is that patience is a crucial virtue when navigating the waters of a new relationship, especially for a Brickhouse who understands her worth. In our fast-paced world, there's often a temptation to rush into intimacy, commitment, and future plans before getting to know someone. However, a Brickhouse knows that building a solid foundation takes time. She tempers herself by embracing the journey and allowing the relationship to unfold naturally, rather than forcing it to progress at an unnatural speed.

Being patient means taking the time to understand your partner's character, values, and intentions. It involves observing how they treat not only you but also others in their lives. This careful observation allows you to assess whether they align with your standards and contribute positively to your happiness. Instead of rushing to define the relationship or putting pressure on yourself and your partner, a Brickhouse remains grounded in the present moment, enjoying the process of getting to know one another.

Most of us were not taught how to date, so it is important to not let your emotions take over. Dating means getting to know someone, often with no references for their character or background. Even potential employers do a background check to understand who they are inviting into their company, so you must also take your time to understand who you are dealing with before committing your life to them. It first takes at least 3-4 months for a man to grow attached to you and then from there, it will take another 3-4 months before you really start to understand who this person is.

Investing at least 6 months into learning the true strength, personality and flaws of a person that you can potentially partner with for the rest of your life is a necessity at this point. Social and mental disorders are on the rise, and you need to take your time to understand who you are aligned with. It is important to remember that who you select as a partner is one of the most important decisions you will make in life, as this person will have a major impact on the quality of life for you and your children. Choose wisely and have patience.

To cultivate patience, continue to live your Brickhouse life by spending time nurturing your passions, pursuing personal goals, and strengthening your sense of self outside the relationship. This will not only keep you fulfilled but also help you maintain perspective.

Communicate openly about your feelings and expectations, ensuring that both you and your partner are on the same page with your desires for the future, whether that be marriage or long-term commitment. Many men and women nowadays are not as focused on getting married but are still interested in a partner to enjoy life with. Either way, you must both have the same expectations.

> I must stress here that having patience at the beginning of a relationship to get to know someone does not equate to waiting years for someone to figure out IF they want a future with you.

Men typically know if you are a woman that they could spend their life with within those first 3 months. If so, he will then confirm with his actions that he has selected you as a life mate and will not want anyone else to snatch you away from him. By year 2 if he is still confused, hesitant or just wants to go with the flow, then you can take that as confirmation that it is time for you to start building your future without him.

Remember, a Brickhouse is not interested in a long-term partnership with just anyone, your happiness is dependent on a partner that is just as invested in creating an abundant life together as you are. Going with the flow for years is not a life plan. Sometimes it may take you walking away for them to understand their loss and come back committed. However, do not allow anyone back into your life without confirmation and commitment to a plan for the future together.

Che' Lovelight

Social Media & Dating

Much of your entertainment and social media feed is full of drama and controversy between men & women, making us believe that dysfunction and tension are the norm, and creating these expectations in our love lives.

Don't let the noise on social media frame your perspective or expectations on dating or relationships. The posts and conversations often highlight extremes, perpetuating negativity or unrealistic standards about men and women. This is why changing your social media feeds to reflect what you desire to bring into your life is an important foundational step in framing the *Brickhouse Mindset*.

There are plenty of pages that cater to happy and healthy relationships, but they may not create the clickbait that these platforms need to survive. This is nothing new. Also, the people in happy relationships are living their happy lives, and most likely want to keep it private and away from the judgmental or envious eyes online.

Social media, while an incredible tool for connection and communication, often distorts our views on reality, especially when it comes to relationships. These platforms thrive on sensationalism, conflict, and negativity because it keeps people engaged and talking, which ultimately benefits the system that profits from our discontent. Every day, we scroll through curated content, absorbing messages that often reflect pain, division, and dissatisfaction more than they celebrate love, healing, and growth.

Brickhouse Relationships

Many of these individuals packaging their pain, blame, and bitterness as wisdom are often playing a role, crafting dramatic narratives to gain followers, go viral, and ultimately profit. Misery loves company, and too often, these discussions foster unnecessary division between people, creating an "us versus them" mentality rather than encouraging genuine connection, empathy, or self-reflection. Worse, this negativity becomes a convenient excuse for bad behavior, enabling people to justify their actions rather than address their accountability.

Attracting and maintaining quality relationships demands more than just longing for connection, it requires a willingness to take responsibility for the energy you bring to the table and the types of people you allow into your life. It calls for honest self-reflection to understand the lessons from past experiences, break unhealthy patterns, and grow into the version of yourself capable of sustaining the relationship you desire.

A fulfilling relationship starts with becoming the person you wish to attract. This means holding yourself accountable, not blaming others for your choices, and refusing to entertain nonsense or compromise your values. It means moving beyond using people to feed your ego or validate a narrative that places all the fault elsewhere. True love and connection require maturity, effort, and alignment, not just with the right partner but also with your own intentions and growth.

Social media might amplify the noise of relationship woes, but you have the power to rise above it by focusing on becoming the best version of yourself and fostering healthy, meaningful connections rooted in mutual respect and accountability.

The next time you come across someone venting about their dating struggles or criticizing the opposite sex, take a moment to seek the lesson. Reflect on where this person might not be taking accountability for their actions and consider how you can choose differently in your own life. Men and women are designed to complement and uplift one another, this is not just human nature but the essence of universal laws. Yet, the division sown by narratives like "I don't need a man" and reducing a woman's desire for stability to that of being a "gold-digger" has spiraled into an alarming cycle of distrust, resentment, and degrading rhetoric from both sides.

Men voicing disdain for women and women expressing disgust for men only serve to deepen the divide, creating a toxic environment where meaningful connection and healing feel out of reach. Let's be clear: this hostility benefits no one.

> As this rhetoric grows, our society is becoming increasingly isolated and burdened with mental health challenges, issues that could be significantly alleviated by choosing to speak to and treat each other, and ourselves, with greater respect and kindness.
> With Love.

This divisive programming doesn't have to define us. Instead of succumbing to a narrative of mistrust and separation, we have the opportunity to rewrite it. Yes, the current climate can lead to further societal breakdown if we allow it, but it also holds the potential to inspire growth, maturity, and self-awareness. Across the world, a quiet revolution is taking place, a growing movement of individuals who are choosing self-improvement over blame, self-love over bitterness, and genuine connection over superficiality. These people are discovering the true value of a loving partnership and are prepared to nurture and appreciate a quality partner when they find one.

This shift is a powerful reminder that while negativity may grab the spotlight, it's the quieter, more intentional efforts toward love, accountability, and mutual respect that will ultimately shape our future. Choose to be part of this movement. Focus on bettering yourself and fostering relationships rooted in care, understanding, and authenticity. This is how we heal ourselves and, in turn, our society.

It is time to shift the focus toward building trust, mutual respect, and shared goals, which ultimately lead to the gratifying partnerships we all desire. Even the angry ones.

> If our society truly valued the well-being of relationships, we would see a greater emphasis on fostering positive, supportive interactions between men and women.

The reality is, men and women need each other, and most of us desire love, connection, and partnership. Just because someone of the opposite sex hurt you doesn't justify harboring resentment toward an entire gender. After all, our parents, siblings, and friends have hurt us too, yet we continue to nurture and respect those relationships. Love deserves the same respect.

Unfortunately, our society often thrives on division rather than unity. Instead of promoting love and connection, it fuels narratives that breed distrust and animosity, ultimately weakening the foundation of our people and families.

The truth is, strong families build wealth, not just financial, but emotional and generational wealth as well. The more divided we are, the more unstable our families become, and the less we are able to secure a prosperous and balanced future. By choosing to embrace respect, understanding, and love, we can defy these harmful narratives and build the kind of relationships and families that thrive despite the challenges society places before us. Let's stop making it harder than it needs to be and start working toward the unity we all deserve. We are generations deep into this divisive programming and we need to recognize it for what it is and work against it.

And, yes, there are many societies that choose to safeguard the family and the way their people interact with media and other social influences. Some call this censorship; some call it protection.

To manifest your best relationships, it's crucial to see through these distractions and focus on what matters to you. Instead of letting media narratives shape your expectations, seek out sources of information and influences that enhance your understanding of relationships and how to better them. By concentrating on what aligns with your values and goals rather than your fears, you can attract more authentic, fulfilling connections.

A Man Will Behave Better When You Demand It

Women are the driving force behind a man's ambitions and achievements. We ignite a passion in them that inspires them to conquer challenges and create stability for themselves and their families.

When we expect less, we get less.

As the womb of creation, we extend our nurturing energy to the men we love, which is why many seek out the nectar of multiple partners until they encounter a woman who inspires them to step up, be their best selves, and by embracing responsibility. When a man meets such a woman, he can elevate from a wandering heart into a devoted partner.

When a man desires a woman, he will go above and beyond to win her over and keep her close. We've all experienced that guy who showers us with the kind of attention and consideration we wish we could get from the man we think we want. Falling in love can happen for many reasons, but it's essential to fall for someone who puts in the effort and shows genuine affection.

When you give your best self to a man without requiring the same from him, you're using that energy in ways that might not serve you or your relationship goals. Men often rise to the occasion when they're held to higher standards and expected to bring their best selves to the table. If you settle for less or tolerate poor behavior, men have little incentive to change or improve. It's important to remember that if a man can receive all the benefits of a relationship without earning them, there's little motivation for him to step up his game.

> ## Men thrive on being challenged and inspired and will often only commit to women who hold them accountable for their actions.

A good man is inspired by a woman who knows her worth and unapologetically sets high standards for herself and those around her. When a woman values herself, she naturally encourages her partner to rise to meet her expectations, fostering mutual growth and respect. This dynamic often explains why it's said that "men love bitches."

The term, though provocative, doesn't mean being rude or disrespectful; rather, it refers to a woman who is confident, self-assured, and unwilling to settle for less than she deserves. She doesn't chase validation or bend over backward to please; instead, she demands effort and reciprocation, knowing her energy and time are valuable.

Men who are ready for meaningful connections are drawn to this type of woman because she challenges them to step up, grow, and be better. She doesn't tolerate laziness, disrespect, or complacency, and this firmness communicates her high value. A man who truly values her will admire and respect her strength, working hard to keep her in his life and grow alongside her.

This isn't about playing games or being difficult; it's about standing firm in your self-worth. By holding your ground and maintaining your standards, you attract partners who respect and align with your values, creating a foundation for a thriving, reciprocal relationship.

Some men are actually disappointed when we don't require their best behavior. They would have given it if we had required it. When expectations are low, it can lead them to believe that winning your affection is easy, which can ultimately reduce their interest.

Remember, do not chase after anyone who's not equally invested in you, and you certainly don't owe a man your time or your body if he isn't treating you in a way that makes you feel desired, appreciated, and secure. A man that is interested in partnering with you will engage with you thoughtfully and respectfully. Until someone shows that he is committed to making you feel valued and secure, focus on dating multiple people (or simply dating yourself) while you build your own best life.

Embrace the *Brickhouse Mindset* by seeking joy, peace, and fulfillment in your own experiences. Even if things don't progress as quickly as you'd like, maintaining this perspective will foster healthy growth in any relationship that's meant for you.

Dating multiple people doesn't mean you have to be intimate with each of them; it's about getting to know different individuals and discovering who aligns with your values and goals. Plus, a little healthy competition can motivate everyone to put their best foot forward. If a man doesn't measure up or isn't offering what you need, don't waste your energy overanalyzing the situation. Acknowledge that he simply isn't the right match for you and move on gracefully.

Che' Lovelight

Wield Your Power Wisely

> I honestly believe that a big reason why the dating pool is so challenging right now is because men like never before have the opportunity to easily bounce from woman to woman to get their primal needs met and this reduces the need for them to present themselves as a quality partner.
> This can be fixed when we women as a collective require the respect and affection that we deserve from men before we gift them with our divine energy.

The dating landscape, which has evolved significantly over the last 70-80 years at most, requires a higher level of discernment than ever before.

Today, we have access to countless potential partners through our expanded footprints and online platforms, while in the past, our options were limited to those within our immediate neighborhoods, tribes or villages. With this increased access, it's even more important for women to be patient and selective about who they allow into their lives.

A woman who values and loves herself will attract a mix of men, both high-quality and low-quality. However, as you deepen your self-love and treasure your worth, it becomes easier to identify which men and situations align with your desires.

It's essential to understand that men are naturally drawn to the feminine energy women exude, a powerful force that goes far beyond physical attraction. Your beauty, nurturing spirit, and potent energy elevate his mood, boost his confidence, and strengthen his masculinity simply through your presence. This feminine energy can inspire and activate him, lifting his spirit and body parts without a single touch! Given the immense allure of this energy, some men take advantage of it if boundaries aren't set. Why would a man walk away from something so delicious if he can enjoy it whenever he wants?

This is why it's crucial for you to establish clear expectations and to carefully discern who is worthy of access to your divine essence. Protect this energy fiercely, and don't hesitate to quickly remove anyone who hasn't earned that privilege. We can't blame our disappointing dating experiences solely on men if we continue to give our time and attention to those who don't deserve it. Value your unique energy, and only share it with those who respect and appreciate it fully.

Even if a man is preoccupied with his career or personal responsibilities, if he values you, he will find ways to reassure you and carve out time for you whenever possible. This is especially true for high-value men, who may have demanding careers that leave little room in their schedules for fun. However, a man who genuinely appreciates you will make the effort to ensure you feel valued and cherished, as he won't want to risk losing you. Remember, it's the quality of that effort that speaks volumes about his feelings.

My Dear Brickhouse, as your self-worth strengthens, so will your standards, guiding you toward partners who value and respect you.

When more women expect and require higher standards, more men will rise to meet these expectations, evolving them all into more thoughtful and responsible partners.

> Men, like women, are increasingly weary of the materialism and superficiality promoted in media; and are also seeking depth, authenticity, and true connection.

As each of us raise our vibration and anticipate partners aligning with our new vibration, we collectively shift the dating culture, creating a cycle where quality companionship becomes the expectation, not the exception. The desire for genuine, meaningful relationships is growing, and together, we're fostering an environment where both men and women can thrive, connect, and find lasting fulfillment.

How a Brickhouse Aligns with What Men Want

It's easy to get caught up in trends and external appearances, believing that physical beauty alone is the key to attracting a quality partner. But true connection runs far deeper. While society often glorifies superficial ideals, the reality is that most men seeking a life partner prioritize qualities that create stability, trust, and emotional fulfillment. As a Brickhouse, you are more than just a beautiful presence, you embody the mindset, confidence, and values that align with what men truly want. By focusing on cultivating your inner strength, self-love, and authenticity, you naturally position yourself as a partner who brings lasting value to a relationship, far beyond fleeting physical attraction.

Consider how the rise of the Badbody ideal recently drove many women to invest in plastic surgery, chasing the trend of exaggerated curves through procedures like BBLs to attract men. Yet, in just a few short years, this trend has faced backlash, with many men now openly criticizing these procedures. This highlights a critical truth: even if you look like society's version of the "ideal partner," it doesn't guarantee that your mind, character, or values will align with a quality man.

In fact, research shows that the physical beauty never tops the list of traits men desire in a wife. Characteristics such as kindness, emotional support, intelligence, and dependability rank as top priorities for men in long-term partners. This is why it is imperative to develop your *Brickhouse Mindset* which naturally aligns with the traits men value most in a partner. This isn't about molding yourself to fit someone else's expectations; it's about stepping fully into your power and becoming the best version of you. When you embrace the principles of the *Brickhouse Mindset*, you elevate your energy and exude confidence, self-respect, and authenticity, the exact qualities that attract and sustain meaningful, lasting connections.

Here is how the *Brickhouse Mindset* aligns with what men want.

1. Confidence: The Foundation of Attraction
Confidence is magnetic. It tells the world you know your worth, and it's a cornerstone of the *Brickhouse Mindset*. Men are naturally drawn to women who exude self-assurance because it signals

emotional stability, independence, and the ability to handle life's challenges. When you cultivate confidence through self-love, goal achievement, and personal accountability, you become someone who stands tall, regardless of external validation. Confidence isn't arrogance; it's simply knowing you are enough as you are.

2. Kindness: A Reflection of Inner Peace
One of the most universally attractive qualities in a partner is kindness. It speaks to your emotional intelligence and your ability to create a warm, supportive environment. The *Brickhouse Mindset* encourages you to release bitterness and focus on healing, allowing kindness to flow naturally from a place of inner peace. A kind woman uplifts her partner, inspires trust, and creates a safe emotional space for growth, qualities any man of value appreciates.

3. Independence: The Power of Self-Sufficiency
Independence isn't about rejecting help or love; it's about knowing you can stand on your own while sharing your life with someone else. The *Brickhouse Mindset* emphasizes self-sufficiency by teaching you to set goals, build a fulfilling life, and take accountability for your choices. Men respect and admire women who have their own passions, goals, and a life they're proud of, as it shows you're not seeking a relationship to fill a void but to enhance an already vibrant existence.

4. Emotional Stability: A Pillar of Healthy Relationships
Let's be real: no one wants to be in a relationship with constant drama or emotional chaos. The *Brickhouse Mindset* equips you with tools like the Passion Pic, positive affirmations, and visualization to manage your emotions effectively. By mastering your thoughts and aligning your energy, you demonstrate emotional maturity, which is essential for building a strong and lasting partnership. A man seeking a meaningful connection values a partner who can navigate challenges with grace and maintain a balanced outlook on life.

5. Physical Attraction: The Power of Taking Care of Yourself
While personality and compatibility are key, physical attraction also plays an undeniable role in relationships. The *Brickhouse Mindset* encourages you to take care of your body, not to meet anyone else's standards but to honor the vessel that carries you through life. When you prioritize your health, fitness, and appearance, you not only feel more confident, but you also project vitality and self-respect. Men appreciate a woman who values herself enough to invest in her well-being.

6. Mystery and Intrigue: Keeping the Spark Alive
The *Brickhouse Mindset* teaches you to curate your energy, focus on your goals, and maintain a sense of individuality. This naturally creates an air of mystery. When you're dedicated to your growth and happiness, you don't need to overshare or prove yourself to anyone. This mystery keeps men intrigued and engaged, as it leaves room for discovery and deepens their respect for your independence.

7. Supportiveness: Building Together
A high-value man seeks a partner who believes in him, encourages him, and pushes him to achieve his potential. The *Brickhouse Mindset* fosters this quality by teaching you to build meaningful relationships rooted in respect and reciprocity. A supportive partner is not a cheerleader on the sidelines; she is a co-creator in building a life of mutual success, happiness, and growth.

8. Accountability: A Marker of Integrity
Accountability is a cornerstone of the *Brickhouse Mindset*. By owning your actions, choices, and emotions, you show integrity and emotional maturity. Men respect women who can admit when they're wrong, learn from their mistakes, and continuously strive to

improve. Accountability builds trust and sets the foundation for a relationship where both partners can grow together.

9. Joy and Positivity: Radiating Happiness
A woman who radiates joy and positivity is irresistible. *The Brickhouse Mindset* encourages you to focus on what makes you happy, to practice gratitude, and to align your life with your passions and desires. When you prioritize joy, you become a source of light and inspiration for those around you, including your partner. Your happiness isn't just attractive; it's contagious.

Selecting a Good Partner

Now that we have got you together, lets get into the details of how to spot a good man. In today's modern dating landscape that is heavily dictated by social media, the conversation often leans heavily toward evaluating a man's financial status rather than focusing on his character, how he treats you, and how well you both support and complement each other. This comical conversation about the prevalence of securing a six-figure man is little more than clickbait because in reality, only about 17% of men in the U.S. earn six figures, which means that if this is your primary criteria for a partner, you're likely setting yourself up for disappointment. Of course everyone wants a rich man, but a suitable partner is someone who can contribute to a lifestyle equivalent to or better than the one you grew up in, or at a minimum better than one that you can create on your own.

While it's easy to be drawn to the allure of a lavish lifestyle that includes luxurious vacations, designer clothes, and fine dining, true happiness and fulfillment run much deeper than financial status. A healthy relationship should be rooted in mutual care, respect, and emotional connection, not just material benefits.

As you navigate your relationship journey, take a moment to reflect: Are you seeking a genuine partner who shares your values and dreams, or are you simply looking for a sponsor to support a particular lifestyle? If it's the latter, that's cool, but it's crucial to be honest with yourself about your expectations. Recognizing this distinction can significantly impact your happiness and the dynamics of the relationship.

The harsh truth is that many women chasing this ideal find themselves alone and disrespected, especially if they expect such a man to also be tall, handsome, faithful and treat them like a true Brickhouse. These men are acutely aware of their desirability, and usually enjoy entertaining their many options, ultimately choosing to partner with their most desired women. Unfortunately, this player lifestyle follows many of them well into older age where they can end up on one of two paths: preferring to date younger women and/or facing deteriorating health and sexual virility. Choose Wisely

When you prioritize money over emotional connection, you may overlook important qualities that contribute to a lasting partnership and your happiness in the relationship, such as trust, kindness, and shared values.

This lack of depth can leave both partners feeling unfulfilled and disconnected. It's essential to cultivate a relationship where both individuals feel valued and supported, contributing to each other's well-being in meaningful ways.

Ultimately, joy in a relationship flourish through mutual investment, care, and compassion. When both partners are committed to nurturing the emotional bond, the relationship can thrive beyond the confines of financial considerations. Prioritizing genuine connection allows love to grow, creating a more profound sense of happiness that money simply cannot buy. By establishing a foundation of respect and emotional support, you open the door to a fulfilling partnership that enriches both your lives, proving that true wealth is found in love and mutual respect.

That said, a man's financial security definitely matters because a Brickhouse invests her own resources into maintaining her abundant lifestyle and allure. Anyone benefiting from her divine energy should also contribute to her well-being. When a partner can't provide for a woman's lifestyle through thoughtful gifts, financial support and shared experiences, it creates an imbalance that can lead to frustration.

A Brickhouse is naturally a giving person, and in an aligned relationship, there must be both giving and receiving. A man who has little to give may eventually become resentful, insecure, or emotionally irresponsible due to his limitations, so this is just not a good situation.

A man cherishes a woman that he loves, but it's essential to understand that cherishing doesn't equate to showering her with lavish gifts.

The true value of a man who wins your heart lies not in his bank account, but in the way he treats you and the efforts he makes to be consistent and ensure you feel special and appreciated.

You should be able to list the ways he enhances your life, creating moments of joy, support, and connection.

Expensive trips and designer handbags may seem enticing, but they lose their appeal when they come from a man for whom spending that money is neither a sacrifice nor a genuine investment in you. A wealthy man who casually throws money around without true intention isn't offering you love or respect, he's simply purchasing your presence. This dynamic not only undermines your worth but also positions you as easily replaceable. The emotional toll of being treated as an accessory can leave you feeling as low as the fleeting highs of the luxury lifestyle once promised.

Similarly, gifts from an average man who disrespects you or fails to prioritize your needs shouldn't secure your affection either. If your focus is solely on the money, then by all means, get the bag. But here, we're building Brickhouses, strong, self-assured women who know they can have it all. We deserve not just a financially stable man, but one who offers his loving intention, heart, affection, and respect. Why settle for less when you are worthy of the full package?

We sometimes find ourselves dating people who cater to our ego or fulfill physical desires, but neglect what matters to our hearts. Your partner should make you feel calm and appreciated, not anxious or insecure. Does he compliment you, offer encouragement for your goals, involve you in his future plans, or find ways to put a smile on your face? These are some of the behaviors, a man can show a Brickhouse that he cares and is committed to nurturing a loving and supportive relationship.

Trust your feelings and intuition; you'll instinctively know when someone's actions and words resonate with your heart. The way they treat others, their choice of words, and their lack of respect for you can raise serious questions about their character. If you had other options, would you still choose them? It's easy to rush into labeling someone as a boyfriend or partner, but if their character doesn't bring peace and value into your life, then you simply may not be aligned.

Ask yourself: Is your time together enjoyable and supportive? Are they contributing positively to your life? Do they take accountability for their actions, responsibilities and decisions? If you find that they are mean-spirited, jealous, selfish, or unavailable when you need them, it might be time to take a step back and reevaluate the relationship. Remember, you deserve a partner who lifts you up, not one who weighs you down.

Ultimately, we're all hoping to find that one special partner to build a life with and share joyful experiences. As you focus on pouring love and positive energy into yourself, and raise the standards you accept from both yourself and others, you will naturally start to attract higher quality individuals who are also doing the work to better themselves. It's crucial to hold yourself accountable to your feelings and standards, and your standards should not just be tall, rich & handsome. The value of a man goes far beyond his height and bank account, it is his genuine desire for you that will provide you with the emotional stability that you ultimately crave.

Additionally, it's important to understand the concept of 'soul ties'. connections occur when we become intimate with someone and spend significant time together, allowing their energy to intertwine with ours, making it difficult to break free. Scientifically, studies have shown that when a man ejaculates into a woman, his semen can stimulate ovulation, induce sleep, enhance feelings of affection, and even reduce depression. This explains why it can take months, if not years, to move on from someone; they're literally ingrained in your system. Recognizing this can empower you to make conscious choices about your relationships and protect your body physically and emotionally.

Your worth is far too valuable to allow anyone to tarnish, delay, or diminish your mental well-being.

By becoming more discerning and demanding more than just superficial attention, you can enhance your dating experiences. Choose wisely and seek out those who elevate your life, dive into the highest-vibing circles that nurture your growth and help you become the best version of yourself!

Checklist for Romantic Partner Selection

In a world where dating and relationships are often depicted as fairy tales or dramatic adventures, it's all too easy to become lost in unrealistic expectations and societal pressures. Learning how to choose a good partner is an essential skill that can profoundly influence our lives. Keep these tips in mind as you navigate the dating landscape with clarity, confidence, and self-respect. Remember, you deserve relationships that reflect your true worth and contribute positively to your journey.

1. Know Yourself First

Before you can find a good partner, it's essential to have a strong knowing of who you are and what you want in a relationship. Reflect on your values, goals, and personal needs. What are your non-negotiables? What are your must-haves and deal-breakers? Knowing these will help you evaluate potential partners more effectively and ensure that you're aligning with someone who complements your life and supports your growth.

- **Self-Reflection:** Spend time identifying your core values and what truly matters to you in a relationship. Consider your past experiences and what you've learned about yourself from them.
- **Self-Love:** Cultivate a strong sense of self-love and self-worth. When you value yourself, and treat yourself well, speak to yourself lovingly and enjoy your own company, you set the standard for how you expect to be treated in a relationship.

2. Look for Compatibility

Compatibility goes beyond shared interests; it involves aligning on fundamental values, goals, and lifestyles. A good partner should be someone who not only complements your personality but also supports your long-term aspirations. Remember, it will be just you and him in the house together for long periods of time. Make sure that you are compatible and are comfortable around each other when no one else is around.

- **Shared Values:** Ensure that you and your partner share core values and life goals. This alignment is crucial for building a lasting relationship that will lead to a happy marriage if that is desired.
- **Lifestyle Match:** Consider whether your lifestyles are compatible. Differences in major life aspects, such as career ambitions, family planning, or living arrangements, can lead to significant challenges.

3. Evaluate Character and Integrity

A good partner's character and integrity are vital for a healthy, respectful relationship. Pay attention to how they treat others, their level of honesty, and their ability to handle conflicts and challenges.

- **Respect and Kindness:** Observe how your partner treats people, especially those who can't offer anything in return. Their behavior towards waitstaff, friends, and family members can be revealing.
- **Honesty and Communication:** A good partner should be honest and open in their communication. Trust is built on transparency and consistent actions.

4. Assess Emotional Maturity

Emotional maturity is a key indicator of a partner's readiness for a committed relationship. Look for someone who can handle their emotions responsibly and engage in healthy conflict resolution. His conflicts can become your conflicts and being with someone that cannot get along with people, including you, can be detrimental to the quality of your life.

- **Self-Awareness:** A mature partner is self-aware and takes responsibility for their actions. They should be able to reflect on their behavior and understand its impact on others.

- **Conflict Resolution:** Observe how they handle disagreements. A mature partner will approach conflicts with a problem-solving mindset and seek resolution rather than escalating arguments or casting blame.

5. Watch for Effort and Investment

A healthy relationship requires effort from both partners. A good partner will show a genuine interest in investing time and energy into the relationship and will actively work towards building a future together.

- **Consistency:** Look for consistency in their actions and words. A partner who genuinely cares will demonstrate their commitment through regular, meaningful actions.
- **Support and Encouragement:** A supportive partner will encourage you to pursue your goals and dreams and will stand by you during challenging times.

6. Trust Your Instincts

Your intuition can be a powerful guide when it comes to choosing a partner. Pay attention to your gut feelings and any red flags that arise during your interactions. Seeing too many red flags is more than enough reason to exit a relationship.

- **Trust Your Feelings:** If something feels off or makes you uncomfortable, don't ignore it. Your instincts are there to protect you from potential harm.
- **Red Flags:** Be aware of red flags such as excessive jealousy, controlling behavior, or lack of respect. These issues can be early indicators of deeper problems.

7. Foster Healthy Boundaries

Healthy relationships are built on mutual respect and clear boundaries. A good partner will respect your personal space, time, and individual needs, and you should do the same for him.

- **Set Boundaries:** Clearly communicate your boundaries and expectations in the relationship. A partner who respects your boundaries is more likely to contribute to a balanced, healthy dynamic.
- **Respect Individuality:** Ensure that your partner values your individuality and supports your personal growth rather than expecting you to change to fit their needs.

8. Enjoy the Journey

Finding a good partner is not just about the end goal; it's about enjoying the journey of self-discovery and connection. Approach dating with an open heart and a positive mindset.

- **Stay Positive:** Maintain a positive outlook on your journey. Each interaction, whether successful or not, is an opportunity to learn and grow.
- **Have Fun:** Enjoy getting to know different people and discovering what you desire in a partner. The process should be enjoyable and enriching.

Selecting a good partner requires self-awareness, accountability, and a sharp eye for character and integrity. By homing in on these qualities and trusting your instincts, you can navigate the dating world with confidence, ultimately finding someone who positively complements your *Brickhouse Mindset*. Remember, a great relationship starts with knowing and loving yourself first, allowing you to reflect the same values you seek in a partner.

Che' Lovelight

While I may not know your specific situation, this guidance aims to equip you for future relationships and assist you in recognizing when it's time to leave a toxic one. If you find yourself in a relationship that brings more pain than joy, the *Brickhouse Mindset* will empower you to evaluate whether you can restore peace and happiness or if it's time to separate and rediscover your own contentment. Sometimes, taking charge of your happiness means clearly voicing your needs and acknowledging that, for both you and your partner, walking away might be the best choice.

Avoid staying in a relationship out of complacency, fear of being alone, or shame.

These feelings should not dictate years of your life, only to lead you to leave for the very reasons you questioned from the start. Instead, focus on becoming your best self and living your best life. In any relationship, challenges and difficulties are inevitable, and I'm not suggesting that my Brickhouses abandon ship at the first sign of trouble. Instead, I encourage you to use your sharpened communication, decision-making, and self-awareness skills to enhance your relationships and thoughtfully navigate your next steps.

Cheating & Unconventional Relationships

The topic of cheating often dominates discussions about relationships, but it doesn't have to be the central focus. When you approach dating and marriage as a true partnership, you realize that to enjoy a prosperous and joyful life, you must align yourself with someone that you enjoy and who matches your vibrational frequency; someone you don't need to change, chase or tolerate. This alignment significantly enhances the quality of your relationship and helps you make better choices in your partner selection.

When you cultivate this level of comprehension, the issue of cheating becomes far less relevant. You'll be engaging with someone who respects you and demonstrates true care and concern for your well-being, which fosters an environment filled with joy and peace. Peace means not worrying about whether he will cheat, not being disrespected by his flirtations with other women in your presence, and not questioning whether he will come home or even call. These behaviors are indicators of a partner who lacks respect and consideration, and such signs suggest that he may not belong in your life to begin with.

Energetically, if your thoughts are consumed by fear of cheating or suspicion of cheaters, you may unconsciously attract those very experiences into your life. As we have discussed, our energy is like a magnet, drawing in what you focus on most. When your vibration is centered on mistrust and fear, you're more likely to align with individuals who reflect that energy.

Your divine energy naturally attracts a range of energies, but by maintaining a high vibration rooted in positivity and confidence, you create alignment with healthy, fulfilling relationships. This elevated state not only draws in what you desire but also empowers you to confidently discern and exclude connections that don't serve your highest good.

In addition, if your primary concern when choosing a partner is whether they've cheated in the past instead of their character, and this singular issue drives you to dismiss them or constantly monitor their actions, you could be setting yourself up for unnecessary loneliness and dissatisfaction. You don't know anything about that relationship and why or when the cheating occurred. You are not that other woman and your connection with this man would be totally different.

Asking someone about past infidelity on a first date and reacting with judgment or disgust creates tension and defensiveness, potentially closing the door on what could have been a meaningful connection.
Just because someone has cheated in a previous relationship doesn't automatically mean they will do the same with you.

It is crucial to heal the fear of cheating before entering a new relationship. Approaching a relationship with suspicion signals to a potential partner that you may still be carrying unresolved pain, which can make you appear vulnerable or insecure. A healthy man may be turned off by you because this signals a lack of trust and emotional readiness, which can make building a healthy connection difficult. Trust is a foundation of any meaningful relationship, and approaching a new partnership with doubt or fear can create unnecessary tension.

Furthermore, he may feel unfairly judged or pressured to constantly prove himself, which could overshadow the natural flow of getting to know each other and building trust organically. Good men are often drawn to partners who exude confidence and emotional stability, as these qualities foster a more balanced and fulfilling relationship.

The wrong man might see your suspicion or insecurity as an opportunity because it suggests you are more focused on proving your worth or seeking reassurance than on setting strong boundaries or valuing yourself. This vulnerability can make it easier for someone with selfish or manipulative intentions to gain control over the relationship.

They may exploit your fear of being cheated on by offering just enough attention or validation to keep you attached, while using your insecurities to excuse their own poor behavior or avoid accountability. For someone with ill intent, your unresolved fears can become a way to maintain power and diminish your sense of self-worth.

When cheating occurs, it is important to understand the reasons behind the infidelity because they can provide crucial insights into whether the relationship can be established or salvaged. Sometimes, infidelity can be corrected by the two partners working together, or it can signal a lack of respect or connection and provides a reason to immediately exit a relationship.

Instead of allowing the act of cheating to be your sole measure of judgment when evaluating a partner, focus on the overall qualities and values they bring to the table. A person's character is defined by far more than their relationship history and reducing them to a single act or label can cause you to overlook important traits that truly matter in building a meaningful connection.

I want to clarify that I am not condoning or promoting cheating in any way; rather, I'm addressing the issue to help you let go of the need to control others through suspicion or the pursuit of a cheater. Entering a relationship with the intent to control a partner is unhealthy and unsustainable, as it stifles individuality, breeds resentment, and undermines trust. If you can't trust someone to respect the relationship, then that's your cue to not enter it, not a sign to tighten your grip.

Remember, your intuition and discernment should guide you, but they work best when paired with a balanced and open mindset. Cheating is a serious issue, but it is not the only factor that determines someone's capacity to be a loving and loyal partner. Focus on building a connection rooted in mutual respect, shared values, and consistent actions, rather than letting fear or judgment block real love and companionship.

Cheating can be an experience or a character trait, this is also why a person's character is of the utmost importance when selecting a partner.

Cheating is a sensationalized issue, overshadowing the deeper complexities of relationships. Some individuals cheat because they lack genuine desire for their partner but choose to stay in the relationship due to the stability, convenience, or benefits it offers.

On the other hand, some people cheat because their emotional or sexual needs aren't being satisfied at home. They seek external partners to fulfill those desires, which can inadvertently preserve the peace and happiness of their primary relationship. In these situations, infidelity might not be a sign of dysfunction; it could be a way to maintain family stability and the desired core relationship.

Since the dawn of time, both men and women have engaged in external relationships and unconventional arrangements. The jokes about the mailman visiting Mommy while Daddy is away or Daddy sleeping with the secretary are rooted in wide-open secrets.

While some couples thrive in strictly monogamous relationships, others find fulfillment in more open dynamics, such as swinging or partner swapping. Whatever couples choose to do within their own relationships should not come under judgement or criticism as we are all individuals and should not expect everyone to live as we do, because often they do not.

Plenty of couples have experienced infidelity and many chose to stay together and will never tell you this. Other people have left a person who cheated in an otherwise happy marriage and regret it for the rest of their life. Each couple and person are individual and there is no one size fits all for relationships despite what you may see in the media.

> Just as there are some people who are fiercely monogamous, there are people on the other side of the spectrum who could never be committed to one partner.

That being said, the conversation around polygamy is more relevant than ever, especially as polygamy gains visibility in today's society. With the rise of this lifestyle, it has become easier for individuals to find partners who share similar desires for non-traditional relationships, allowing them to cultivate happiness together. However, this arrangement hinges on open and honest communication about needs from the very beginning. If one partner is interested in exploring multiple relationships, they need to be upfront about it.

Conversely, if you're not comfortable with that dynamic, it's crucial to be honest with both yourself and your partner, and to step away from any situation that doesn't align with your values. Never compromise your true self just to keep someone else in your life, as doing so only leads to self-betrayal and potential heartache. Prioritizing your own needs is essential for genuine fulfillment and happiness. The other person is, and so should you.

Polygamy, when rooted in mutual respect, shared values, and genuine love for all involved, can be a harmonious and fulfilling lifestyle choice. However, in this country, it is often bastardized by individuals who exploit the concept for sexual gain rather than approaching it with true love and integrity. Some men use polygamy as an excuse to satisfy their greed or inflate their egos, rather than fostering meaningful, aligned relationships with multiple partners. This can lead to emotional harm, manipulation, and imbalanced power dynamics.

For these reasons, entering into a polygamous relationship requires extreme caution, deep self-awareness, and a clear understanding of the intentions and values of everyone involved. True polygamy demands transparency, equality, and emotional maturity, not selfishness disguised as a lifestyle choice.

In many cultures, polygamy is completely normal, with men of stature often having multiple wives as part of their lifestyle. This idea that we must be eternally devoted to just one partner is really more of a societal expectation than a universal truth. Societal norms are ultimately constructs, shaped by cultural, historical, and social factors that shift over time. They're "made up" in the sense that they represent collective beliefs rather than universal truths. What's considered "normal" today might change tomorrow, which underscores that we're free to define our own path, independent of societal expectations.

We're increasingly getting an inside look at the dynamics of high-profile marriages, revealing that what happens behind closed doors often defies our assumptions. For instance, Bill Gates vacationed annually with his ex-girlfriend. Warren Buffett and his wife even formed a trio with another woman at his wife's request. Celebrities like Will and Jada Smith, Dolly Parton and Angelina Jolie have all openly acknowledged their experiences with non-traditional and open relationships.

There are many aspects that can contribute to unconventional marriages beyond adding partners. For instance, the husband may take on the primary caregiving role while the wife is the primary breadwinner. Some couples choose to sleep in separate beds, and in other arrangements, spouses maintain separate residences but are fully committed to each other. Nowadays it is becoming more common for ex-couples to choose to live in the same home after divorcing in efforts to provide stability for their children.

An unconventional marriage is one that defies traditional norms and expectations, focusing instead on the unique needs, values, and desires of the couple. Rather than adhering to a prescribed script of what marriage "should" look like, an unconventional marriage allows partners to create a bond that reflects their individual personalities and shared goals.

> If we are being honest, the picture that society paints of marriage is not always a happy one, so you should do all you can to create one that is.

Ultimately, you're entering into a partnership with another individual, and what unfolds between you is deeply personal. It's vital for both partners to enter this relationship with a genuine desire to love, support, and build a fulfilling life together. What that life looks like is unique to the two of you. As your marriage evolves, so will each of you as an individual. Sticking rigidly to a single expectation of yourself or your partner limits growth.

As you work to build your own Brickhouse life in a way that resonates with you, approach your marriage and relationships with the same level of honesty and openness. Instead of fixating on the possibility of cheating, prioritize character and shared goals. Focus on cultivating a partnership that fosters compassion, trust, and mutual respect, allowing your relationship to grow and thrive on a foundation of authenticity and love.

Understanding Narcissism in Relationships

Infidelity was a reality in my marriage on both sides. He had long been cheating, and towards the end of our relationship, I found myself having an affair with the only man who could make me stray. This was someone I had loved in my youth, and when he reentered my life just as my marriage was crumbling, it felt like an incredible whirlwind to ease my escape.

Ultimately, I chose to leave my marriage not because of the cheating, but because the underlying issues that existed before we even said "I do" had never been resolved. I had married a malignant narcissist, and the infidelity was merely the cherry on top of a much larger, toxic sundae. Digesting the characteristics of narcissism is not just a form of self-protection; this is vital information to prevent you from being dominated by those that do not have the capacity to love you.

As an empath and a lightworker, I have attracted numerous narcissistic personalities throughout my journey and chose to align myself with them. I emphasize that this is a choice, as it is essential to understand that you hold the power to determine who you allow access to your divine energy. Both light and dark energies are drawn to your vibrant spirit, making it crucial to familiarize yourself with the traits of darkness. By doing so, you can safeguard your heart, mind and quite tragically even your life from those who may seek to drain your energy and diminish your well-being.

Narcissism, often characterized by a lack of empathy, an inflated sense of self-importance, and a lack of compassion, can create significant emotional turmoil and confusion.

These behaviors are often covers for their severe lack of self-love and jealousy. I have had two narcs confirm this to me. One confessed to being jealous of me, admitting he made things difficult because I "always got my way." Another said he was envious of the peace and balance I radiate. I never knew that men could be jealous of women and now understand that these behaviors are classically narcissistic.

A lack of empathy is a failure to understand or care about your feelings. When you express sadness or frustration, they may dismiss your emotions, respond with indifference or focus instead on their own needs. Manipulation is another hallmark; narcissists are skilled at twisting situations to serve their interests, creating false truths that make you question reality, or they may use guilt or emotional blackmail to control you. In a relationship with a narcissist, the dynamic typically revolves around their desires and needs, leaving little room for your own. If the relationship caters to their interests without considering yours, it's a significant red flag.

At the beginning of a relationship, a narcissist may shower you with attention, creating an illusion of deep connection. However, this behavior often diminishes once you are emotionally invested, leading to feelings of confusion and insecurity. Even if the attention is sustained, you must understand the difference between attention and affection. Affection is more intimate than attention. Affection involves feelings of warmth, tenderness, and fondness towards you. This can be conveyed through physical touch, such as hugs, kisses, holding hands or cuddling on the couch; as well as kind words and surprising you with thoughtful gestures that express love and care.

I stress the importance of knowing the difference between attention and affection, because this is a covert tool utilized by many narcs.

My ex-husband and I were joined at the hip until our daughter was born, but he rarely extended any affection beyond a peck on the lips, eventually descending into an asexual relationship. In addition, the relationship was severely one-sided which is another key characteristic, and I experienced virtually all the other narcissistic tactics listed below in abundance. I tolerated it because we were best friends, generally enjoyed our time together, and were in business together but this did not equate to a romantic nor emotionally supportive relationship. We were friends and business partners that should have left it at that.

I've experienced more than my fair share of belittlement and a lack of sensitivity from men attempting to undermine my self-worth to control me. If I shed 60 pounds, it was not enough because my body was not firm. If I was corporate fly, I was not music industry fly. Oh, and I cannot forget that on multiple occasions I was told that I was "too pretty", and that was used as a justification for the lack of compliments that every woman needs to hear from her husband.

If you're questioning whether you are in a narcissistic relationship, pay close attention to the signs I'm sharing. Each of my narcissistic relationships had exciting upsides that initially overshadowed the underlying issues. I largely laughed off the things my partners said to me, understanding that their behavior was basically them showcasing their own wounds. Wounds that I thought that I was built to withstand. If anyone could tolerate these personalities, it was me. I also did not believe the things they said to me, so my self-esteem protected my self-confidence. I have long had a general definition of narcissism, but it was still challenging for me to admit to who I was dealing with, until I made the conscious decision to love myself and acknowledge that I deserved more.

If you find yourself facing similar struggles, I encourage you to use this book to help rebuild your self-worth and formulate an exit strategy, as change is unlikely. Experts on narcissism will tell you that the only viable option is to leave; these individuals often lack the self-awareness required to alter their harmful behaviors. Ultimately, the responsibility to take the necessary steps to save yourself rests solely on you. No one else can dictate when it's time to go, that realization must come from within. Ask Spirit for confirmation and do not ignore it.

It's natural to feel hesitant about leaving someone who brings excitement, a common trait among narcissists, but you must arrive at a point where you can recognize your self-destructive patterns and demand more for yourself. You deserve peace, true love, and adoration.

It's essential to remember that experiences with a few difficult partners should not taint your perception of all men. There are many quality men out there who have found themselves caught in unfortunate relationships or involved with female narcissists, and they, too, are in search of peace and genuine love. You may find yourself viewing nice guys as dull, especially after being attracted to the excitement of darker energies. However, as you awaken to the beauty of peace and authentic affection, you'll begin to appreciate these qualities far more than the fleeting thrill that chaos can bring. With this newfound perspective, you'll have a blueprint to build a fulfilling life with a new partner, one that focuses on valuing tranquility while cultivating joy and meaningful experiences together.

Examples of Narcissism in Relationships.

Narcissists often exhibit a range of behaviors in relationships that can be harmful and manipulative. Here are some common traits and actions associated with narcissistic individuals:

- **Gaslighting**: This involves making the victim question their reality or perceptions. A narcissist might deny events, twist facts, or manipulate situations to make the other person feel confused or insecure about their memories or feelings.
- **Love Bombing**: In the early stages of a relationship, a narcissist may shower their partner with excessive affection, attention, and gifts. This intense idealization can create a sense of dependency and attachment, making it harder for the partner to see any red flags.
- **Criticism**: After the initial idealization phase, a narcissist may start to belittle, criticize, or demean their partner. This shift can leave the victim feeling unworthy and questioning their self-esteem.
- **Projection**: Narcissists often project their own negative traits or behaviors onto others. For instance, if they are dishonest, they may accuse their partner of being untrustworthy, deflecting attention away from their own issues.
- **Blame Shifting**: Narcissists rarely take responsibility for their actions. Instead, they will shift the blame onto their partner,

making them feel guilty for things that are not their fault. This can create a toxic cycle of self-doubt and guilt.
- **Playing the Victim**: When confronted or challenged, a narcissist may play the victim to gain sympathy or manipulate others into feeling sorry for them. This tactic deflects responsibility, and redirects focus onto their perceived suffering.
- **Silent Treatment**: This tactic involves ignoring or refusing to communicate with someone as a form of punishment. It creates an emotional vacuum that can leave the victim feeling anxious and desperate for reconciliation.
- **Triangulation**: A narcissist may bring a third person into the relationship dynamic to create jealousy, competition, or division. This tactic reinforces their control by pitting people against each other.
- **Boundary Violation**: Narcissists often disregard personal boundaries, believing they are entitled to take what they want from others. This can manifest in physical, emotional, or psychological invasions of privacy.
- **Entitlement**: Narcissists believe they deserve special treatment and may become angry or dismissive when they don't receive the attention or privileges they feel entitled to.
- **Self-centeredness**: Narcissists often display extreme self-centeredness, prioritizing their own needs, desires, and feelings above anyone else's.
- **Isolation**: Isolation is another significant tactic employed by narcissists. They may subtly or overtly attempt to cut their partner off from friends, family, or support systems, creating a sense of dependency on the narcissist.
- **Withholding**: Narcissists withhold affection, communication, or support as a way to manipulate their partner into compliance or to punish them for perceived slights.
- **Dismissing Feelings**: Narcissists often belittle their partner's feelings, making them feel invalidated and unimportant.

- **Grandiosity:** This is a key characteristic of narcissistic behavior, manifesting as an inflated sense of self-importance and an exaggerated belief in one's abilities, talents, or achievements.

Understanding these behaviors is crucial for recognizing the signs of a narcissistic relationship. A narcissist is incapable of loving you properly and the only way to better your situation is to leave for your mental and emotional well-being. When discussing challenges within a typical relationship, it is important to first voice your concerns before leaving, but in a situation with a narcissist that demonstrates more than a handful of these tactics, I am certain you have already exhausted communication and become numb to your needs. The only option is to leave as they do not have the capacity for self-awareness or love.

If you find yourself feeling drained, manipulated, or consistently unhappy, it's crucial to take action. Remember that staying in a relationship out of fear of being alone or shame can lead to prolonged unhappiness as well as mental and physical health challenges. Make a plan for your future that focuses on your peace, happiness and fulfillment.

Manifesting Love with the Brickhouse Mindset Framework

A fulfilling and loving relationship is a desire that holds a top spot on the hearts of many women, which is why I've devoted a significant portion of this book to guiding you in identifying and building the healthiest, most rewarding connections. Using the Brickhouse Mindset Framework, you'll learn to align your energy, thoughts, and actions to manifest the partner and relationship you truly deserve and/or better the one that you are already in.

Code-Switch: Redirecting Your Focus to Love

Remember, it starts with mastering your thoughts. If you're constantly thinking, *there are no good men left* or *what if I get hurt again?* —guess what? You're setting yourself up to vibrate at a frequency that keeps attracting those very fears. The first step is to stop giving power to those doubts and fears. That's where Code-Switching works its magic.

When negative thoughts creep in, and you find yourself spiraling into fear or self-doubt, catch them. Close your eyes and imagine a moment with your dream partner. Picture yourself walking hand-in-hand, laughing, or sharing a quiet moment filled with love and connection. Feel the warmth of that love as if it's happening right now. Hold this vision for at least 20 seconds, allowing it to fill your heart and elevate your energy. The more you practice this, the more natural it becomes to shift your vibration from worry to joy, to focus on love and possibility instead of fear and lack. This is the first step in attracting the relationship you deserve, vibrating with its energy before it even arrives.

Feed: Nourishing Your Mind with Healthy Perspectives

What you feed your mind will either help or hurt your journey. Let's be honest, scrolling through endless social media posts about "toxic men" or sitting in conversations that bash relationships does nothing for your vibe. These things may seem like harmless entertainment, but they subtly shape your beliefs about love and partnership.

To align with a healthy relationship, begin curating what you feed your mind. Start feeding your mind with content that inspires and uplifts you. Change your social media feeds, read books, watch movies, and listen to podcasts that showcase healthy relationships. Surround yourself with people who talk about love in a way that feels good and motivating. Seek advice from the couples and married people in your life. Ask them how they got together and what keeps them together. By feeding your mind with these positive examples, you reshape your belief system and set the stage for the kind of partnership you want to manifest.

Affirm: Speaking Love into Existence

Words have power, my dear Brickhouse. If you keep saying, *I'll never find the right one* or *All men are trash,* you're writing a script for your life that the universe is happy to follow. You are mentally reinforcing those narratives and attracting the experiences that validate them. Flip the script and affirm what you truly want.

Every day, speak affirmations that align with the relationship you're manifesting. Say, *I am worthy of a love that respects and cherishes me. I attract a partner who matches my energy and effort.* Visualize that affirmation becoming reality. Write it down in the Dating Journal below and/or purchase one on my website. Speak your desires into existence and let them sink into your subconscious mind. The more you say it, write it, and feel it, the more you are programming your brain and the universe to attract the relationship of your dreams.

Believe: Trusting in the Love You Deserve

Belief is the cornerstone of manifestation. You have to *know* that your ideal partner exists and that the universe is already working to bring them into your life. This belief isn't about wishful thinking; it's about embodying the certainty that you are deserving of love.

Visualize your dream relationship as if it has already happened. Imagine the joy of waking up next to your partner, the deep conversations you share, and the adventures you experience together. Feel the gratitude of having this love in your life. When doubt creeps in, remind yourself that divine timing is at play and trust that the universe knows exactly when and how to deliver.

Brickhouse Relationships

Becoming the Love You Seek

Let's be clear, this framework isn't just about attracting someone else. It's about becoming the woman who is ready to receive the love she deserves. Elevate your energy by embracing self-love, setting boundaries, and cultivating a joyful, fulfilling life on your own. When you pour into yourself, loving yourself, respecting yourself, and living your best life, you naturally attract someone who matches that energy.

This is about more than just getting into a relationship; it's about alignment. It's about taking accountability for the energy you bring into a relationship and the people you choose to allow into your life. By practicing Code-Switching, Feeding, Affirming, and Believing, you're not only attracting love, you're attracting the right kind of love.

Your dream partner is out there, searching for you just as much as you're searching for him. Trust the process, trust yourself, and trust that the universe is working in your favor. Remember you're a Brickhouse, baby! You're not just manifesting love; you're manifesting the most fulfilling, empowered version of yourself. And that is the greatest gift you can bring to any relationship.

Homework

Using a dating journal can be incredibly beneficial for a Brickhouse for several reasons. I love these so much I have also created a catalogue of more detailed Dating Journals you can buy on my website to best support your experiences. Before you head out on your next date, take a moment to fill out the **Dating Desires** section in the **Brickhouse Dating Journal** below. This will help you gain insight into your own values and clarify the qualities you desire in a potential partner and relationship.

After each date, set aside time to complete the **Post-Date Overview** so you can process your thoughts and feelings while they're still fresh. This reflection is essential for interpreting your feelings and processing your thoughts about the encounter.

Periodically review your entries to identify patterns in your dating experiences. Look for common themes in your feelings, the qualities of the people you date, and any recurring red flags. This reflection will help you understand your evolving desires and standards.

If you later find yourself feeling anxious because of a lover's behavior, pull out your journal. Use it as a tool to reassess your emotions and gain perspective. Sometimes, a reality check is all we need to maintain our Brickhouse status. Remember, it's important to stay true to yourself and keep your eyes and ears open to the reality of your situations and what you're experiencing.

By following these steps, your dating journal will help you navigate your dating journey with intention and self-awareness, ensuring that you're aligned with what truly matters to you.

Brickhouse Dating Journal

Dating Desires

- These are the ideal qualities I am seeking in a partner.
- These are the qualities and gifts I have to offer a partner.
- What is my most desired quality in a partner and why?
- What are my non-negotiables?
- What is my dating end goal?
- How does my ideal partner make me feel?
- What kind of family background do they have?
- If he has children, is this desired or a deal breaker?
- What kind of lifestyle would they lead for ultimate compatibility?
- Describe an ideal date.
- Am I open to touching on the first date?
- Am I open to kissing on the first date?
- Am I open to sex on the first date?
- What do I want to learn about this person on the first date?
- What hobbies would I love them to enjoy?
- What information do I need to keep to myself until I get to know them better?

Dating Affirmations

Now, write your own dating affirmations describing the type of healed divine partners you attract and how these suitors make you feel.

Post-Date Overview

Complete this overview of the date soon after you return home.

- Name
- Age
- Birthday
- Occupation
- Date location?
- Children, Yes/No. How many?
- What did I like about them?
- What I liked about the date?
- What did I not like about them?
- What did I not like about the date?
- Did I feel comfortable being myself around this person?
- My ideal next date?
- Questions to ask on the next date?
- How do they compare to my ideal partner?
- What will I do to distract me from creating a fantasy surrounding them? What is my Passion Pic and focus for the upcoming week?

What are my main takeaways from this date? (Lessons learned, things to improve upon, etc.)

Brickhouse Relationships

A Cautionary Tale

Maybe it's my high vibes, laid-back demeanor, and non-judgmental understanding of people, but for some reason, the men I've allowed into my life seem drawn to spend lots of time with me, even if deep down some of them have secretly despised me. It's all too easy to get entangled with someone who wants to keep you close, even if they have no desire to fully love you or help you reach your full potential.

This is why it's essential to pay close attention to a person's energy and how they interact with others. Dark energy is difficult to hide; jealousy, insecurity, and bitterness often slip out in subtle and obvious ways. A Brickhouse naturally attracts both light and dark energy, so it's vital for her to surround herself with people who uplift and empower her, especially when it comes to intimate partners. By choosing to be around those who radiate light and positivity, she protects her own energy and ensures that her ambitions and happiness aren't overshadowed.

Twice, I allowed myself to be thrown off course by "love." The first time, I veered off my own path and onto my ex-husband's, thinking it would accelerate my dreams. In some ways, he did push me forward, but in many others, he worked tirelessly to crush my spirit and ultimately broke my heart in a way you could never imagine.

This man was mentally abusive, using a range of tactics to break me down and keep me small while I fully supported him. Even though I fought him every step of the way, the constant drama and challenges between us, and he with other people just became too much. He knew how to isolate me, planting seeds of doubt to keep me under his control and make me distrust almost everyone else. I believed I had high self-esteem and thought I could withstand his narcissistic behavior, but I've come to realize that, while I may have had high self-esteem, I lacked self-love and true self-worth, which are even more essential.

Once I woke up and realized that although I did not ask for nor require much, I indeed deserved much better than what I was receiving, I left him. I had allowed myself to be drained, disrespected, and used by an opportunist. By then, he had been unfaithful for some time, and toward the end, I stepped out as well. We were essentially living separate lives, he was rarely home, and I later found out that so much was happening behind my back. After 13 years together, I made the decision to pack up my home within three days and leave, reclaiming my life and the respect I had long been denied.

Looking back in hindsight, I saw the signs early on that should have kept me from attaching myself to this man, and this is why I urge you to pay attention to red flags and remove yourself early. Learn from the stories you've heard, the lessons that others have taught. When someone, especially a partner shows a lack of character, accountability, disrespects you, or tries to control you, know that this is not love.

It took me three years to finally pull the plug. I had started the work to regain my *Brickhouse Mindset*, and I knew the relationship was beyond repair. I asked Spirit for confirmation, and the very next day, he picked a ridiculous argument over a cell phone charger. In that moment, I knew I was done. I told him I wanted a divorce. Less than 30 minutes later, he told our five-year-old daughter, on her first day of kindergarten, that Mommy was breaking up our family. There was no going back after that. I was stunned that his first reaction was to hurt our child and pull her into the end of our marriage.

It was the confirmation I needed, a sign I could no longer ignore. In that moment, I finally understood the meaning behind "when a woman's fed up, there ain't nothing you can do about it." When I left, I left for good, fully embracing my decision to reclaim my life, my peace, and my strength. When you ask Spirit for guidance, trust that you will receive it, but it's up to you to accept that truth and act accordingly.

His behavior became diabolical after I left him, revealing the full extent of his cruelty. So much has transpired, but I will keep the details brief to focus on the most critical and tragic lesson. Even before our divorce, he had been overindulging our daughter and refused to discipline her, painting himself as "Nice Daddy" and me as the "Mean Mommy." For the last 2 years of our marriage, he was rarely home, claiming he was "working" to get his career back on track after tanking two businesses. Meanwhile, I had returned to corporate sales and was rebuilding my career to support our family. He insisted that since I had been able to reestablish my career, I should allow him the same opportunity. His only responsibility during this time was to take our daughter to and from school. Virtually every day, as soon as I returned home from work in the evenings, he would leave and stay out all night, returning only in time for school drop-off in the morning.

During their time together, he constantly spoiled our daughter, showering her with gifts every day on the way home from school. He undermined my authority as a parent, frequently rescuing her from time-outs and reprimanding me in front of her without even asking why she was being disciplined. This created an environment where I was constantly undercut, leaving me frustrated and powerless in my own home.

When I finally moved out after he reneged on our agreement that he would move out, he filed for divorce within two weeks. Before I moved, we had both agreed that the end of our marriage was mutual, and we had taken shared responsibility for its demise. However, after I left, he refused to speak to me and became obsessed with making my life miserable. He moved back to his mother's house, which was over 40 miles away from me and thought it was perfectly fine to have our daughter travel an hour and a half each way just to get to and from school on public transportation, since he refused to get a job, car or a driver's license for years.

This later caused her to be deemed truant by the state because she missed an excessive number of days when she was with him. I repeatedly asked him and the courts to change the parental visitation so that our daughter could stay with me during the week so she can get to school within 15 minutes; but he fought me on everything just so that I wouldn't have a second more time nor authority over him. He went so far as to call Child Protective Services and the police, falsely accusing me of child abuse.

This was the first of the most incredible betrayals I experienced. I had always parented gently, to the point where my own friends and family often criticized me for not being strict enough. His accusations were baseless and cruel, and I later learned that calling CPS is a common tactic in contentious divorces, often weaponized to inflict pain rather than protect children.

The CPS worker quickly realized the tragic dynamics at play and scheduled a meeting, outside of his normal responsibilities in efforts to mediate a resolution for our family. However, after a particularly argumentative conversation, he expressed his frustration and acknowledged his inability to find common ground. Thankfully, the case was closed but the damage to our already fragile co-parenting relationship was just warming up.

After achieving Chairman's Club at my job in NYC, I was offered a promotion to manage the Atlanta territory, I was elated. Everyone in my company worked remotely, so me living in the territory was not mandatory, but it was strongly suggested that I do. Being that my ex-husband had chosen not to work for over 3 years, plus the list of parenting infractions I continued to endure, I knew that the court would allow me to move with our daughter to Georgia. I was wrong. The court has strict 50/50 custody guidelines and after waiting over 9 months for a decision, I was not allowed to move her out of the state. The judge specifically said, 'you can go, but she has to stay here". I was wrecked. After all I had suffered and achieved, I knew this move and opportunity was the fresh start I desperately needed.

To make matters worse, after my court defeat, I was informed that I needed to relocate to Atlanta or risk losing my position. This was just after Covid, and the company decided it was time for sales executives to significantly increase in-person interactions with clients. Revenue wasn't meeting expectations, and with tighter expense budgets and shifting rules, the pressure was on me. Losing this job, a role I excelled in and loved would have been devastating, not just for me but for my daughter as well. The prospect of her having two unemployed parents was unthinkable.

My ex-husband, however, refused to negotiate a new parenting plan or even discuss my move. He was determined to block me at every turn, especially knowing that my relocation to Atlanta would place me closer to my boyfriend. What made this situation even more surreal was how the promotion seemed like divine intervention. It came out of the blue after I met the Atlanta director during my Chairman's Club winning trip to Maui. At the time, I believed the stars had aligned to offer me an escape from the chaos I was drowning in, a chance to reclaim my peace and build a better future.

About that boyfriend... Just as my marriage was unraveling, a man from my past, the one I had always believed to be my soulmate, reached out to me through social media. From the moment we reconnected, it was as if time had stood still. He was everything I remembered and more. Even as a teenager, I knew he was special, a god in my eyes, my Twin Flame. The first moment I saw him all those years ago, he captivated me completely, mind, body, and soul.

For decades, he remained "the one" in my heart, the person I unconsciously measured everyone else against. Reconnecting with him felt like stepping into a dream, one that awakened all the feelings I had tucked away, feelings that reminded me of the love and connection I had always longed for.

When he reentered my life, his brilliance fed my soul like no one else ever had. Nearly fifty years old yet radiating a timeless beauty that would stop strangers in their tracks. I often would sit quietly, watching him, marveling at one of God's most beautiful creations. He was finer than fine and we were on the phone day and night, fueling this bond that seemed unbreakable, yet he carried lessons of his own.

Our intimacy was electrifying. Every sexual encounter was intense, and would last literally for three hours straight, unlocking my deepest traumas, as he narrated my past hurts from childhood to adulthood as if peeling back layers of my psyche in some kind of primal therapy. It was a strange form of healing, an ecstatic purge that had me releasing my pain in waves of pleasure and tears.

He was a master of the body, knowing exactly how to evoke ripples of orgasms. His approach was a perfect blend of rough and sweet, teasing and pleasuring, a lover skilled in every way. He was a man of wealth and power and lived halfway across the country. He would fly me monthly to our meeting place in Atlanta, and for days leading up to our encounters, he would prepare me for the lessons at hand. He created a curriculum for each visit, using our intimate moments to prepare me for the battles I was facing. Coaching me on how to stand strong in the courtroom for my divorce and advising me on the high-stakes negotiations in my corporate deals. Offering me encouragement in the most intimate ways, whispering words of admiration and celebration in between breaths, feeding the validation I had craved for so long.

But this was his web, woven carefully to keep me bound to him forever, and be a "good girl for Daddy". His presence was hypnotic, like something written in the stars, a love story reincarnated, glorious and consuming. Yet beneath the allure, it was a case study in mental warfare, a relationship that felt otherworldly but was ultimately designed to control me, to keep me anchored in his world by the force of his seductive influence. It was passion and power entangled, a connection that both lifted me up and threatened to trap me within his complicated reality.

The relationship was intensely cerebral, emotionally vulnerable, and healing all at once. He seemed to know me better than I knew myself, and that was part of the problem. This man was an energy vampire. He studied me, kept close tabs on my every move, monopolized as much of my time as possible, and I was more than willing to give it to him. We stimulated each other's souls, minds, and deepest desires, addicted to the connection that bridged the darkest and lightest parts of ourselves.

He triggered my unresolved "Daddy Issues", and I ignited his "Mommy Issues" from a mother who had ingrained in him a disdain for "fat chicks" Although I had lost over 60 pounds and was looking good by the time we reunited, we were lovers in my youth, and he admitted that, when we first met, he'd felt cursed because the girl who could be "The One" wasn't his idea of perfection. And yet, despite it all, we were drawn by an undeniable magnetic pull between us. I loved him like I'd loved no other, and he loved me in the ways he was capable of. Together, we were a beautiful contradiction, intoxicating yet destructive, healing yet harmful, bound together by passion and our own broken pieces.

He sparked a realization in me: although he made me feel incredible, he was actively trying to extinguish my dreams and bind me to a situationship where I'd always come up short. I could have stayed, convinced I was happy, indefinitely. But we were vibrating on completely different frequencies. He rejected spirituality yet clung to me for the peace he couldn't find elsewhere. His life was a whirlwind of chaos and drama that had nothing to do with me, yet I kept him grounded. I was a bright light in his miserable world. He called me his muse yet despised the divine energy that fueled my spirit.

See, he married another woman shortly after reaching out to me on social media, just after I got myself together and admitted that my marriage was beyond repair. My divorce was inevitable and ultimately necessary, and his reentry into my life brought a relationship that seemed to offer almost everything I thought I wanted.

Never in a million years did I picture myself as someone who would cross the line into infidelity, but he was that one. When they say the devil knows exactly how to tempt you... they aren't lying. We spent four years together, and despite our intense connection, I never worked to disrupt his marriage. Instead, I focused on helping him become a better husband, encouraging him to see his marriage from a wife's perspective. Yet, no matter how much effort I poured into supporting him and navigating our complicated bond, the highs and lows of his life spilled over into mine, and once again my life was being overshadowed by a man.

About halfway through our relationship, I began stepping into my purpose by starting this book. I had always known I was meant to write it, and after navigating the trials of divorce and the complex chapters of my life, the words began to flow with a clarity I hadn't expected. *Brickhouse Mindset* became both a sanctuary and a mission, a way to process my journey and share it in a way that could inspire and guide others. It was during this time that the disparity in our frequencies became glaringly apparent.

Being bound to his charisma was not only intoxicating but also stifling. He wanted me tethered to him, constantly available, and focused solely on his needs and desires. The relationship, while deeply passionate, became a cage, one that kept me from healing, evolving, and pursuing the divine calling that had been whispering to me for years.

I felt torn, knowing I was in a relationship that filled me with both immense joy and pain, not only because he was married but because we were spiritually misaligned. As I got deeper into my writing and spirituality practices, I turned my focus inward, nurturing my well-being and igniting the flame of self-love. With this shift, his cynicism and superficiality grew sharper and became impossible to ignore.

He ridiculed the book I was pouring my heart into, and dismissed my pursuit of spirituality entirely, as if my growth and self-discovery were somehow trivial or misguided. He often talked about how spiritual people were always broke, belittling the journey that was bringing me closer to peace and purpose. I got to the point where I stopped talking about the book with him because the mounting disrespect was hurtful.

Meanwhile, my ex-husband was relentless in his torment, creating constant co-parenting drama that drained my energy and left me feeling despondent. I was desperate for peace, for clarity, for a way out of the turmoil that surrounded me. When I was told I had to relocate to Atlanta or risk losing my job, the weight of it all nearly broke me. The move felt like an insurmountable challenge, a crossroads I wasn't sure I could navigate.

Once again, I cried out to The Divine, pleading for guidance. I surrendered completely, releasing my fears and asking Spirit to illuminate the path to peace. In that moment of surrender, I chose to trust that the answers would come, even if I couldn't yet see how. Then, in a moment of piercing clarity, Spirit spoke to me with unmistakable guidance: *"move to Atlanta, allow your daughter to live with her Dad, but you gotta let go of Him."* I immediately understood this as a test of my devotion; to God, to myself, and to my higher calling. It was a challenge to demonstrate my commitment to the life I was being called to live. Trusting in the divine wisdom that had brought me to this crossroads, I surrendered to the message and obeyed. It was a profound moment of alignment, one that marked the beginning of my journey toward my purpose to heal and to teach.

This powerful command urged me to break free from the toxic entanglements that had held me captive for far too long. It was a call to liberation, a chance to embark on a profound journey of self-discovery and healing. It also compelled me to make one of the most selfless and heart-wrenching decisions of my life: to honor my daughter's desire to spend more time with her father.

The decision was incredibly painful. Many times, when she returned to me from his home, she would cry to go back. Despite pouring every ounce of love and affection into her, I couldn't help but feel rejected. One day, she told me with all the innocence of a child, "It's not that I don't love you or want to be with you, I just love being with Daddy." As difficult as it was to hear, I understood.

I had witnessed her bond with her father countless times, and I knew that although we were close, she was indeed a Daddy's Girl. I convinced myself that this decision would make everyone happy, even if it nearly broke me in the process.

Allowing my daughter to live with her father was an unthinkable decision, one I never imagined I'd have to make. Yet, after countless heartfelt conversations with her, where I explained my plan to travel back and forth every month so we could still spend meaningful time together, she consistently agreed. In this arrangement, I envisioned finally becoming "Nice Mommy," free from the constant conflict and drama that had consumed the last two years of our lives. I imagined weeks filled with joy, bonding, and quality time, untainted by the tension of our previous living situation.

With that decision, I chose to move to Atlanta, and step away from a relationship that no longer served me. I chose walking away from my dream lover even though I would now live in his city. The most beautifullest thing in this world loved me but would never be in love with me, and it was sucking my heart and potential dry. I walked away for me and also so that I could eventually be available for the man that wants me to be his number one. This is how you choose yourself and step into your power, by giving up the things that are keeping you from having what you deserve and being your best self. This is the same reason I left my husband.

My focus shifted to building a stable and fulfilling life not only for myself but also for my daughter, a life anchored in peace and the hope that this sacrifice would ultimately support her well-being and happiness. To maintain my presence and my motherly responsibilities, I arranged to fly back home monthly, staying with my mother for a week at a time. Her home was close to where my ex and our daughter lived with his mother, allowing me to remain actively involved in my daughter's life despite the distance. I would go from having her two weeks out of the month to just one week, a week that would be filled with love, joy and unforgettable memories.

I found strength in recognizing that, throughout history, countless parents have faced the heart-wrenching decision to leave their children for work, driven by the need to create stability, opportunity, and a better future for their families. And they didn't have FaceTime. Military personnel endure deployments that last months or even years. Entertainers and athletes travel extensively to honor their contracts, journalists chase stories around the globe, and traveling nurses or sales professionals spend long periods away from home to meet the demands of their careers.

When my ex-husband refused to negotiate with me, I sought legal counsel. The lawyer bluntly acknowledged the reality of my situation, telling me I was "dealing with an asshole" and advising me to move forward with my relocation and file a motion to revisit the custody arrangement. It was a painful but practical path, and I truly believed I was making the best decision for my daughter's future. Even though it pained my heart to leave, I clung to the hope that this sacrifice would ultimately provide her with the stability and opportunities she deserved.

Never in my worst nightmares did I imagine that this decision would result in being separated from her for well over a year. After I moved, my ex refused to communicate with me or let me speak with our daughter. He ignored my calls, FaceTimes, and texts, and without warning or notice, he secretly moved her out of state. For over 6 months I did not even know where she was living. This is an extreme case of parental alienation and parental abduction, where a child is taken or concealed by one parent in violation of state law and the custody rights of the other parent.

This affects over 200,000 children each year, and you would think this mostly happens to fathers, but the National Center for Missing & Exploited Children states that fathers are the most common abductors. I could never have imagined being at the center of an unbelievable custody battle, fighting to see the child that I brought into this world, nursed for over three years, and lovingly indulged, in the hopes of fostering a deep and unbreakable bond with her.

For over a year and a half, I've been separated from my daughter, and I am now battling through the courts to have justice served. This situation is not just hurtful; it is deeply devastating for both me and my child. Neither of us deserves the pain and heartbreak it has caused. My empathetic heart once made me believe I could endure and navigate life with a malignant narcissist, but this experience has been a harsh and unrelenting lesson in the danger of ignoring red flags.

I never wanted my daughter to grow up having to recover from her parenting. The internet is flooded with stories of adults grappling with the scars of damaging words, neglect, and abuse inflicted by their parents; wounds that often shape their lives long into adulthood. I was determined that my daughter would never have to share such a story. I always spoke affirming words to her, nurturing her greatness and creativity while shielding her from the pain of physical and emotional harm.

Despite my efforts, the person who was supposed to partner with me in creating a beautiful life for our child has worked tirelessly to undermine it. Some may judge my decision to step away from her daily life as negligence, but it was a decision made out of immense love for her. I made the painful choice to provide for her in a way that I believed would bring her happiness and stability.

I pray every day that the incredible love I have for her, combined with the spiritual, healing, and self-love practices I've embraced, will help her heal and thrive when we are reunited. A mother's love is undeniable, a force of nature that transcends distance, and I believe it has the power to overcome even the greatest of challenges. My loving energy and unwavering commitment to her well-being will prevail, helping us both move forward with strength and grace.

I can say with full confidence that the tragedy I have endured has also become the foundation of my greatest transformation. I am leaning deeply into the principles of the *Brickhouse Mindset* to safeguard my mental and emotional well-being as I navigate this indescribably painful chapter of my life. Writing this book amid such turmoil has not only helped me heal but made me stronger while reaffirming my mission, which is to share these tools with you. I am walking fully in my own power, embracing my purpose, and trusting the divine path Spirit is leading me through. I embody this framework not just as concepts, but as daily practices to maintain my sanity and find moments of joy each day.

I have grown to love myself in ways no one else ever could, embracing my independence, authenticity, and the woman I was always meant to be. I've learned to prioritize my peace, to protect my energy, and to nurture the life I deserve. I dove headfirst into self-discovery, peeling back the layers of pain and doubt to reveal the strength, wisdom, and resilience that had always been within me. This journey has shown me that even the most painful situations can lead to the most beautiful new beginnings. I know what I was called to do, and the steps flawlessly aligned for me to be a healer and teacher.

What's more, I've been blessed to attract some incredible people into my life, individuals who vibrate with my spirit, share my values, and uplift me with unwavering support. These relationships have been a gift, affirming the importance of surrounding yourself with those who see your light and encourage it to shine brighter. Their presence has been a reminder that love and connection are not just possible but abundant when you align with your true self.

****

My Dear Brickhouse, I share my cautionary tale as a heartfelt warning: stay far away from narcissistic men, no matter how charming, accomplished, or appealing they may seem. The consequences of entangling yourself with someone who thrives on manipulation, control, and selfishness are not just painful, they are unimaginable.

A narcissist doesn't just break your heart; they dismantle your sense of self, exploit your vulnerabilities, and leave chaos in their wake. For me, it went beyond emotional abuse, it resulted in the unthinkable: being estranged from my own child. My former best friend, husband, business partner and the father of my child became my biggest adversary, weaponizing the most precious bond of my life against me.

The signs were there, but like so many of us, I ignored the many red flags, believing I could handle him, believing I could endure. Don't make the same mistake. Pay attention to how a man treats you, speaks to you, and respects your boundaries. A narcissist will always reveal himself, and it's up to you to walk away before you're too deeply entangled. Protect your peace and your future, don't give them the power to define your story.

- Chapter 14 -

A Brickhouse Marriage

Brickhouse Mindset Shift: A marriage is a business partnership not a wedding.

A Brickhouse marriage is defined by reciprocity and mutual support, creating a partnership where both partners actively contribute to each other's happiness and well-being.

It's about pouring into one another, ensuring that life is not only manageable but also joyful as you work together towards common goals such as peace, stability, and a happy family. When you approach dating with the *Brickhouse Mindset*, you lay the foundation for a successful marriage by choosing someone who genuinely cares for you and your aspirations. I have already laid out some great insight to help you best select your partner in life, and now I would like to help you design a rewarding marriage by discussing a few things that are often overlooked when planning for a potential union.

I want to emphasize that just as life is filled with its ups and downs, intense challenges will also be present in marriage. Arguments, disagreements, feelings of loneliness, and periods of boredom are all part of even the healthiest marriages.

It's crucial not to enter marriage with the misconception that it will be your source of happiness, as your happiness is your responsibility.

Instead, view it as a partnership with someone who can hopefully help make navigating the complexities of life more manageable and enjoyable.

Many women grow up dreaming of their wedding day, eagerly anticipating the moment they marry the love of their life. Yet, all too often, they aren't prepared for the realities of marriage; the hard work and dedication it requires to keep that love thriving. At its core, marriage is a business partnership; it's an agreement to better each other's lives and achieve mutual goals. Your shared vision for the future should focus on creating a relationship that benefits both partners, one in which you both are willing to roll up your sleeves and work together, especially during challenging times.

Effective communication is a cornerstone of a successful marriage. It's essential that both partners have honest conversations about what marriage means to them, how they will co-parent, divide household responsibilities, and plan for the future. This open dialogue not only fosters understanding but also helps to align your expectations and visions for your life together.

Embracing Brickhouse behavior means engaging in relationships that encourage your growth as a woman while also valuing what you contribute to the relationship and your partner's life. It's essential that both partners feel appreciated and valued in the partnership, cultivating an environment where loving energy flows freely between you. Demonstrate your appreciation for his presence in your life, his feelings, and what matters to him, just as he should for you. If this mutual respect and support are lacking, ask yourself: why are you even thinking about marriage?

> A marriage should enhance your life, adding the benefits of companionship, respect, and financial partnership.
> Being in a marriage without these components could be detrimental to your life.

Reflect on the countless couples who are married yet miserable. They may have tied the knot with someone who makes them feel trapped rather than alive, possibly choosing a partner who acts more as a dependent or opponent than an ally. The person you marry will significantly impact your quality of life, peace of mind, and overall happiness. Therefore, it's crucial to select your partner wisely and to engage in thorough discussions about what your marriage will look like.

When considering a life together, it is necessary to discuss how both partners will manage the day-to-day responsibilities of the household. This includes practical matters such as cooking, cleaning, and maintaining the home. Establishing a clear plan for who will take on these tasks, and how often, sets the stage for a balanced partnership. Will one of you be responsible for meal prep while the other handles grocery shopping? How often will cleaning take place, and what cleaning tasks will be shared? These discussions not only help in dividing responsibilities fairly but also foster teamwork and cooperation, ensuring that both partners feel valued and engaged in the daily workings of their shared life.

Even if the two of you are already living together, before entering into marriage is the perfect time to redesign your lifestyle together. After all, a marriage is a contract, and this contract should be thoroughly discussed and negotiated.

When conversations arise about why marriages fall apart, the focus often leans toward major issues like infidelity or outright unhappiness. However, the real culprits are frequently the small, everyday frustrations that accumulate over time, leading to significant rifts between partners.

It's crucial not to overlook the seemingly minor responsibilities and habits when discussing your needs and expectations within a marriage. Often, once a couple ties the knot, individuals tend to settle into their established routines even more firmly. The belief that "I've secured this person, so they must be content with who I am" can lead to complacency in the relationship.

This is precisely why it is essential to engage in open and honest discussions about your needs and expectations before entering marriage. Don't make assumptions about how life will unfold after the wedding. Moreover, marriage can shift dynamics, particularly for men who may become more territorial regarding their wives and children. Post-marriage, they might expect you to be more present at home and available to meet their needs. This expectation could lead to feelings of confinement or dissatisfaction if your personal goals or desires for independence clash with these newfound responsibilities.

If he was controlling, distant, or disrespectful before the marriage, those behaviors are likely to intensify once you tie the knot.

What you were willing to tolerate for a year or two can quickly become a heavy burden on your mind, body, and soul, robbing you of the peaceful and healthy life you deserve. The patterns established before marriage don't magically disappear; instead, they often solidify, making it even harder to address those issues once you're committed. Recognizing these red flags early on is crucial because they can significantly impact your overall well-being and happiness in the long run. Choosing not to marry can sometimes be a healthier option, especially if the relationship dynamics are already not what you desire.

    The choice of a life partner and potential father of your children is not one to be taken lightly. This person is a representation of how much you value yourself and will significantly impact your happiness and by extension, your children's well-being. Beyond discussing the number of children you want, it's essential to explore how you wish to raise them. What are your views on discipline? Who will handle daily responsibilities like diaper changes, feeding, and school drop-offs? Do you desire to be the "Soccer Mom" or homeschool? What does dating and curfew look like for your teenager? Don't just discuss the immediate needs of your new family, think long term.

> In addition, women around the world have the support of multiple generations in the same house and/or have nannies and maids as a regular part of family life to provide relief and support.

This is not a lifestyle set aside just for the rich, it is just more expensive here in the USA. Maintaining full-time work and a household, especially with multiple children, can be physically and mentally exhausting. Will you require a nanny or an occasional housekeeper to support you? Will your mother or sister need to move in to help? These are all valid questions.

Do not feel the need to be Superwoman and do it all alone.

Your partner cannot expect his woman to maintain the traditional roles, especially if he is unable to maintain the full financial responsibilities that created balance in that dynamic for prior generations.

We need to move past idealistic expectations and design a family that is successful, and that takes teamwork. In America, we are just now acknowledging the stress the modern household weighs on women and relationships, so we need to plan better for everyone's betterment. Women are natural nurturers, and more times than not, it's the woman who shoulders a heavier load in maintaining the household and raising children, regardless of the initial plan. If you find yourself in a situation where your partner isn't fairly sharing responsibilities, it can lead to resentment and frustration within the relationship. We must learn from these challenges and design ways to avoid them in the future. A modern household requires both partners to contribute to all aspects of the family and home upkeep. Even stay at home moms need a supportive partner.

> When considering marriage, it is even more vital to consider your partner's character carefully. Ask yourself, do you want your children to be shaped by this person's values?

Will he be a supportive co-parent who respects your decisions, or might he undermine your authority? Will he set the tone for a loving and respectful family environment by respecting you in front of your children and requiring that your children respect you as well?

Financial goals are another crucial area to discuss when planning your life together, which goes beyond who is paying what bill. This conversation should encompass not only your long-term aspirations like a home and retirement plans but also practical matters like vacation plans and how to pay for your children's education, which need to be agreed upon and budgeted for. Additionally, it's essential to align on the lifestyle you both aspire to achieve, as well as how you'll work together to make it a reality.

These financial and lifestyle aspects significantly shape the fabric of family life. If either of you has professional ambitions, it's important to discuss how you can support one another in reaching those goals. Open communication about your financial situations, including debts and future aspirations, fosters transparency and trust.

By establishing a comprehensive plan for the success of your family that ensures both partners feel secure and supported, you're laying the groundwork for a healthy and thriving partnership. Addressing these topics together strengthens your bond and helps you navigate the complexities of shared life more effectively.

Many marriages fail because of a lack of finances which can lead to not only hardship but also a lack of respect. Ideally, it's best that you marry someone that can help provide a lifestyle like the one you grew up in and/or better than the lifestyle that you can provide by yourself. Gender roles are evolving, and women no longer need to shrink themselves as we are no longer entirely dependent on our partners for financial support. Most households require both partners to contribute financially, making it essential for both individuals to have a voice and share responsibilities.

In any healthy relationship, it's essential to recognize that balance does not always mean equality; rather, it involves acknowledging and valuing the unique contributions each partner brings to the partnership.
Both individuals can contribute to maintaining a thriving relationship by fostering an environment of mutual respect and support.

Emotional intelligence plays a significant role in maintaining this balance. Each partner should strive to understand not only their own feelings but also the emotions of the other. This understanding cultivates empathy and compassion, allowing partners to respond thoughtfully to one another's needs. For example, recognizing when one partner is feeling overwhelmed can prompt the other to offer encouragement or take on more responsibility in certain areas, reinforcing the partnership without the need for direct requests.

Additionally, each partner should express appreciation for the other's contributions, however big or small. Acknowledging the efforts made, whether it's emotional support, problem-solving, or simply being present, strengthens the bond and fosters a culture of gratitude within the relationship. When both partners feel appreciated, they are more likely to continue putting in the effort required to nurture the relationship.

Both partners should be open to growth and adaptation, because as individuals, your needs and circumstances will evolve, and it's crucial that you remain flexible and willing to reassess the roles in the partnership. By maintaining a mindset of cooperation rather than competition, partners can navigate challenges together, ensuring that both feel valued and respected.

Marriage is definitely not a solution to loneliness, and catching a man is not your end game. Your love goals are best centered around securing a mutually beneficial relationship with someone who will work as hard as you to build an enjoyable life together and push forward with you when things are not ideal.

> Remember, God is love, and the love you seek in a partner should primarily bring you joy, security, and appreciation.

We often fall in and out of love with various people throughout our lives, and sometimes we find ourselves entangled with individuals we believe we love but who actually do not enhance our lives. We might feel obligated to stay due to the time and emotion we've invested, or because of shared familial ties, business relationships, or friendships that surround us.

But let's be real. Many of us endure situations we wouldn't dare to admit to our friends or family. When the going gets tough, it's often just you and your partner facing the challenges alone. Potential embarrassment or the expectations others place on your relationship should never outweigh your need to feel loved, safe, and appreciated in a marriage.

If you're in a relationship where the future stability of your family hinges on your partner's potential, such as if he's focused on his education or building a business, and you are currently supporting him financially and emotionally, it's even more critical that he already shows up as a dependable, appreciative and loving partner. Otherwise, if the relationship doesn't last or he doesn't meet the expectations, you may find yourself feeling deeply disappointed, as your sacrifices and patience go unrewarded. Your happiness and peace should never be based on someone's potential; instead, they should be rooted in the reality of who your partner is today and the respect, love and stability they bring to your life now.

Without the foundation of mutual respect and love, you might often feel anxious or undervalued. These feelings can build up over time, making it hard to enjoy your life together. You might hold onto the hope that things will get better, believing that love will fix everything. But if the core issues like poor communication or emotional disconnect aren't addressed, those problems are likely to persist. Eventually, you might reach a breaking point where you realize you need to leave to reclaim your happiness.

Staying in a relationship that doesn't serve your highest good can lead to more heartache than being single. While being alone can feel lonely at times, being stuck in a relationship that brings you down can feel even worse. You might find yourself giving so much of yourself while receiving very little in return. That emotional toll can leave you feeling isolated, even if you're not technically alone.

> Entering a marriage with a person that you are not aligned with, or one that challenges your peace and happiness, can not only lead to disappointment but can also push you to later leave for the same reasons that upset you in the beginning.

Then you will have lost years of peace, possibly your health, and have children who are now affected by these decisions. Recognizing that being single can sometimes be healthier than being in a relationship that doesn't uplift you can empower you to make choices that honor your well-being and happiness. Ultimately, it's about knowing your worth and choosing relationships that enhance your life.

Open and honest communication with your partner is essential for fostering a healthy and fulfilling relationship. It's important to feel comfortable expressing your concerns, needs, and desires with the person you've chosen to share your life with. Many individuals find themselves unhappy in their relationships simply because they struggle to be truthful with themselves and consequently, with their partners.

When you share your thoughts and feelings openly, you create an opportunity for empathy and connection. Too often, unspoken expectations and unaddressed issues can lead to resentment and misunderstandings. By being forthright about your needs and desires, you pave the way for more meaningful conversations that can strengthen your bond.

Your man cannot read your mind, nor can he fix problems that he is not aware of. Do not let bitterness build up because you do not want to hurt your partner's feelings discussing things that may make you uncomfortable. You are walking around with hurt that could be corrected with conversation. If you cannot open up and speak freely with someone you are in a lifelong relationship with, where are you relating? How are you better and/or free in this relationship? Be honest and face challenges.

Open communication in any relationship should be a bare necessity. If you feel mostly obligated to stay in the relationship, just don't want to start over or feel that you cannot do any better, rather than a pure sense of eternal love and devotion to this person, you may be robbing yourself from the person out there that can give you this. Eternal love and devotion is in the Universe for you if you choose it. This alone should be your motivation to never settle. Question and work on yourself until you attract the person that is aligned with your needs in a partner. Period Brickhouse.

As a Brickhouse, seeking guidance from The Divine when approaching marriage is a powerful step toward creating a fulfilling and harmonious partnership.

This process begins with cultivating a deep sense of self-awareness and clarity about what you desire in a relationship. Before making such a significant commitment, take the time to connect with The Divine through prayer, meditation, and quiet reflection.

In these moments of stillness, ask for wisdom and insight into your heart's true desires. You might inquire about the qualities you seek in a partner and how you can align your actions with the values you hold dear. Seek clarity on whether this potential partner complements your journey and supports your growth. By opening your heart and mind to Divine guidance, you allow yourself to receive messages that resonate with your higher self.

Trust that The Divine will provide the answers you need. Sometimes, this guidance may come as a gentle nudge, a feeling of peace, or even signs in your everyday life. Pay attention to your intuition, as it often serves as a bridge between you and The Divine. When doubts or fears arise, remind yourself that it's okay to seek reassurance and clarity from a higher power.

Remember that a Brickhouse marriage is rooted in mutual respect, love, and compassion. By inviting The Divine into your decision-making process, you ensure that your union is built on a solid foundation that honors both your needs and those of your partner. Embrace the journey with faith and confidence, believing that The Divine is always guiding you toward the life and love you deserve.

Homework for Singles

Here are some questions that you can answer for yourself and discuss with your partner before considering marriage. Think carefully about these questions to get a full picture of the kind of marriage and family life that you desire. You can create this with the right partner who is on the same page as you. If you two do not align on many of these areas or you get a dissatisfied feeling from your partner's answers, you may need to reconsider marrying this person.

I am sure these conversations will bring out many emotions and truths. Pay attention to the small voice in your head and be honest with what you are hearing. Once you marry someone, you are most likely cementing a lifelong relationship with this person. Look at their character, the type of person they are, how they treat you, how they treat other people and themselves, how they make you feel and your romantic attraction to them. If you have any fear of this person not treating you well, not upholding their responsibilities or agreements, not being financially and emotionally balanced in a way that will enable them to fulfil your unified vision, please think seriously about marrying them. If you were to ask divorced women and men how they felt at the time of their marriage, many will say they had reservations in the back of their heads. Don't be us.

Questions to Ask a (potential) Fiancé

- Describe your ideal marriage.
- Describe your ideal family life. Daily Life? Spiritual Life?
- What roles and responsibilities do you feel a husband must fulfil?
- What are your thoughts on parenting and how do you envision raising children?
- How do you envision dividing household responsibilities?
- What is the best way for us to handle conflicts or disagreements that come up?
- How important is personal space and alone time to you?
- Where do you see our family in five years? Ten years?
- Is there anything that I need to know about you and/or your desires before we get married?
- What are your biggest fears or concerns about marriage?
- How can we keep the love and spark alive?
- What role do you see our families playing in our marriage?
- Do you want to live here for the rest of your life? If not, where else interests you? Why?
- What are your plans for retirement?
- How important is it for us to have regular check-ins about our relationship?
- Would you be dedicated to a mutual plan for our lives together?

Homework for those in Marriages

If you are married, below is a list of questions that you can ask your partner in efforts for both of you to grow closer and more connected. It is important that you communicate with each other to build trust, deepen intimacy and resolve any issues before they become insurmountable mountains. Marriage is a journey of growth and development for both individuals and the relationship itself. This exercise is also a way to chip away if not resolve any conflicts you are currently experiencing.

By asking thought-provoking questions, couples can explore new ideas, set goals together, and support each other's personal and relational growth. As time passes, people change, and so do their needs, desires, and perspectives. Regularly checking in with each other ensures that both partners are on the same page and understand each other's evolving thoughts and feelings.

- What are our biggest dreams and aspirations for our relationship and family, and how can we work together to turn these goals into reality?
- What are some of our favorite shared experiences or adventures we've had together, and how can we continue creating memorable moments?
- What do we value most about each other and our relationship?
- How can we prioritize quality time amidst our busy schedules?
- How can we improve our communication to ensure we're both heard and understood?
- What are some of our personal fears or insecurities, and how can we help each other alleviate them?
- What are some of our fears or worries about our relationship, and how can we address them together with compassion and understanding?
- How do you feel about how we handle conflicts?
- Is there anything you would like to change?

A Brickhouse Marriage

- How can we continue to grow and evolve as individuals and as a couple, while nurturing our connection and love for each other?
- How do you feel about the way we share responsibilities for family obligations?
- How do we feel about our level of intimacy and emotional connection, and what steps can we take to deepen our bond even further?
- Are there areas in your life where you feel you need more support from me?
- What are your personal goals, and how can I support you in achieving them?
- How can we express gratitude for each other more regularly?
- How can we ensure that our marriage remains a priority as life changes?

My Closing Message

As I bring *Brickhouse Mindset* to a close, I want to express my deepest gratitude for joining me on this transformative adventure. It has been an absolute joy to share these empowering insights and practical strategies with you, all crafted to help you simplify the art of loving yourself and living your best life.

I wrote *Brickhouse Mindset* to make your life experiences easier by weaving together universal principles, timeless self-love practices, and effective strategies for self-mastery. My hope is that this guide acts as your personal owner's manual, helping you navigate life's twists and turns with greater ease, while sparing you from the struggles that I and many others have faced. Remember, life is fundamentally simple, and the quicker you align your choices with your true goals and desired feelings, the more fulfilling and joyful your life will be.

I was built to withstand the pain I experienced, but that doesn't mean I deserved it. In a way, I feel like I signed up for this challenge long before I came to this earth. Deep down, I've always known I was meant to be a blessing to the world. I vividly remember sitting atop a mountain on a bicycle with someone I didn't know, someone I probably haven't even met yet. As we looked down at the neighborhood below, I said, "Let's go help these people", and we rode down the mountain.

That moment encapsulated my purpose; I've always believed that sharing my experiences could uplift others. This understanding has anchored me through trauma after trauma. From a young age, I knew

My Closing Message

that God didn't send me here to suffer, and I clung to the belief that one day Spirit would rescue me and grant me what I truly deserve.

My saving grace has been the realization that to whom much is given, much is expected. True teachers and healers endure pain because it's through these lessons that we can teach. It's through the journey that we can guide others. It's through the pain that we can heal. Not everyone is called to be a teacher or healer, but if you feel that pull, be prepared for intense challenges. The key is to navigate those trials with resilience and emerge as an inspiring example, rather than a cautionary tale.

As you work toward becoming your best self, you'll naturally inspire those around you to do the same. This creates a beautiful ripple effect, where one person's growth leads to another's, and together, we can uplift each other. By raising the vibrations of happiness, peace, achievement, and love within our families and communities, we create a world changing impact. This is how I aim to fulfill my dream: by inspiring millions of Brickhouses to embrace self-love and create the lives of their desires.

Brickhouse Mindset is here to remind you that you are a powerful manifesting goddess. When you cherish the fact that you are a goddess of love who deserves to be loved, your life will manifest your greatness. You'll feel better about yourself, make decisions that honor your worth, and attract better people and opportunities into your life. With this belief, you'll find it easier to make choices that align with your highest good and bring you closer to the life you desire.

I pray that *The *Brickhouse Mindset* becomes a tool for millions of women (and men) to gain control of their minds and navigate their way out of darkness. If this book helps you take the reins of your life and fulfill your purpose, then I have truly served mine.

****

Now, as you join me in this life improving journey to always choose to become our best selves, I'd like to leave you with some friendly reminders:

1. You Hold the Key
The power to shape your destiny lies within you. Your thoughts, actions, words, and beliefs are the magical ingredients that craft your life experiences. The *Brickhouse Mindset* equips you with the tools to unlock that potential. Speak, think, and act as if you already have the life you desire, for your words and thoughts are the architects of your reality.

2. Reach for Your Light
When sadness, doubt, or anxiety cloud your mind, remember to reach for your Passion Pic, that vivid, joyful image of your dream life, or simply focus on the next better feeling. Shift your energy by visualizing what excites you, brings you peace, or makes you smile. Each small step toward joy lifts you closer to the vibration of love and fulfillment, reminding you that even in difficult moments, you hold the power to guide your emotions and realign with your Brickhouse energy.

3. Cultivate Joy
Finding joy in everyday moments builds emotional resilience, making it easier to navigate life's challenges with grace. When you allow yourself to enjoy life's simple pleasures, you elevate your energy, attract positive experiences and manifest your desires. It is

My Closing Message

one of the most powerful ways to raise your vibration and align with the energy of abundance, peace, and happiness. Whether it's laughing with a friend, dancing to your favorite song, or simply appreciating a beautiful sunrise, these moments of joy build a foundation of emotional strength and create a ripple effect of positivity in your life. Cultivating joy daily is both a practice and a reward; embrace it and let it lead you to the life of your dreams.

4. Banish Negativity
Protect your mind and spirit from negativity and fear. Remove toxic influences, whether they come from people, media, or self-doubt. Replace them with uplifting energy that fuels your dreams. Shift how you view challenges and visualize your solutions with confidence and optimism. Clear your inner world of shame, lack, and self-criticism, for they hold no place in the life you are building.

5. Develop a Relationship with Spirit
Strengthen your connection with God/Spirit by creating a spiritual practice that resonates with you. Access divine guidance through prayer, meditation, journaling, and quiet reflection to find peace and clarity. Trust that when you ask Spirit for help, the answers will come, often through signs, intuition, or unexpected opportunities. By listening and following where you're led, you align yourself with divine timing and step closer to your true purpose.

6. Embrace Growth
Growth often comes hand in hand with obstacles. This discomfort is like the cocoon that transforms you into the beautiful butterfly you aspire to be. Challenges are not roadblocks; they are steppingstones on your path. Every step forward, no matter how small, is a victory. Embrace these moments as opportunities to rise above and grow stronger.

7. Trust the Process

Building your Brickhouse lifestyle isn't a one-time task; everything unfolds in divine timing. Trust that every step, even the challenges, are guiding you toward your highest good. Stay patient and open, knowing the universe is aligning opportunities to match your energy and intentions. Every day, you will be presented with choices, those that move you toward your dreams, those that pull you away, or those that leave you stagnant. Choose wisely. By consistently applying the principles you've learned, you will continue to evolve, adapt, and refine your life.

8. Rest and Reset

Rest, self-care, and balance are vital to maintaining your high vibration. Incorporate meditation, relaxation, and rejuvenating activities into your lifestyle. Schedule in fun, massages, date nights, girls' nights, spiritual baths, walks in nature, and fasting. We are not here simply to work; we are here to fulfill our purpose by vibrating high and enjoying a life that attracts the things that align with that purpose. Burnout lowers your frequency and diminishes your ability to learn and grow from life's lessons. Regularly recharge, reflect, and reassess where you are on your journey to ensure you remain aligned with your purpose.

9. **Believe in Yourself**

    Brickhouse, have unwavering faith in your abilities. You already possess the potential to create the life that you desire. By consistently aligning your actions with your dreams, you weave a future that reflects your true power and vision. Speak to yourself with kindness and encouragement, affirming your worth and capability every day.

My Closing Message

10. Be Grateful
Gratitude is the soil where your dreams take root and flourish. By nurturing a grateful heart, you invite abundance, positivity, and fulfillment into your life. When you appreciate the blessings of The Divine, both big and small, you align yourself with a frequency of abundance. Gratitude shifts your perspective from scarcity to overflow, opening the door for even greater blessings to flow into your life.

11. Choose a Partner with Strong Character
The character of your partner profoundly shapes your life and future. A person's integrity, honesty, and emotional maturity are far more important than surface-level traits or fleeting chemistry. A partner with a strong character will respect you, support your growth, and bring stability and trust into your life. When you align with someone who reflects your values and honors your worth, your relationship becomes a source of strength and peace rather than turmoil. Conversely, choosing someone lacking in character can drain your energy, create unnecessary drama, and hold you back from your purpose. Remember, a partner is not just someone to share your life with, they influence your emotional well-being, your dreams, and the legacy you leave. Choose wisely, and build a life that thrives on mutual respect, love, and integrity.

12. Love Yourself Fiercely
Loving yourself is not a luxury, it is your responsibility. You are the foundation of your own happiness, and no one can take better care of you than you can. By loving yourself, you set the tone for how others treat you and create a life rooted in respect, peace, and fulfillment. Taking care of your mental, emotional, and physical well-being isn't selfish; it's necessary. Feed your mind with positivity, nurture your body with rest and nourishment, and protect your spirit by setting boundaries and prioritizing your peace. When you love yourself fully, you honor the Divine within

you and empower yourself to create a life that reflects your worth. This is your greatest responsibility and your greatest gift to yourself and the world.

The Importance of Maintaining Your Mental Wellness

Maintaining mental health is essential to living a balanced, fulfilling life. It affects every aspect of our existence, from how we think and feel to how we handle stress, make decisions, and build relationships. In the wake of the COVID-19 pandemic, we are finally beginning to recognize the critical importance of mental health. Yet, despite this growing awareness, mental health continues to be overlooked or stigmatized, leaving many individuals, particularly women without the tools, resources, or support necessary to thrive.

Women disproportionately face mental health challenges, with higher rates of anxiety and depression compared to men yet are less likely to prioritize their well-being due to societal norms that encourage selflessness and resilience at any cost. The average woman juggles numerous roles: mother, daughter, partner, professional, and friend, all while battling societal pressures to look, act, and live a certain way. This relentless pursuit of perfection often leads to burnout, self-doubt, and feelings of inadequacy. Add to this the emotional labor women frequently perform, managing household responsibilities, nurturing relationships, and supporting

My Closing Message

others, and it is no wonder so many women experience mental health challenges.

Approximately **1 in 5 women** in the U.S. experience a mental health condition each year. Anxiety disorders, the most common mental health issue in the U.S., affect **23% of women compared to 14% of men.** Depression also affects women at **twice the rate of men**, with nearly **10% of women** experiencing a major depressive episode annually. Additionally, **postpartum depression** affects **1 in 8 mothers** in the weeks and months after giving birth.

Women are more likely to experience trauma-related mental health issues. Statistics reveal that **1 in 3 women** worldwide have experienced physical or sexual violence, events that significantly increase the risk of developing anxiety, depression, or PTSD. These statistics illustrate the compounded challenges women face due to societal, biological, and relational factors.

Despite these numbers, many women go untreated. Among women experiencing depression, nearly **50% do not seek professional help,** often due to stigma, lack of resources, or caregiving responsibilities that make it hard to prioritize their own needs.

The challenges women face are real, but with the *Brickhouse Mindset*, you can rise above the noise and build a life rooted in joy, purpose, and mental clarity. By focusing on self-love, cultivating peace, and nurturing a positive outlook, women can overcome societal pressures, heal from trauma, and thrive. Mental wellness is a necessity, and the *Brickhouse Mindset* provides the tools to support it.

Che' Lovelight

"You Owe it to Yourself to Live Your Best Life!", Che' Lovelight

The *Brickhouse Mindset* isn't just a philosophy; it is a call to action. It's a pledge to simply love yourself and live your best life, one that harmonizes with your deepest desires, ambitions, and the Divine Spirit.

As you close this book and venture into the next chapter of your life, I encourage you to carry these principles with you and make them an essential part of your daily existence. Embrace your incredible potential, love yourself, have confidence in yourself, and persevere through any challenges that come your way.

I wish you boundless success, enduring happiness, and a life filled with joy as you shape the future you've always dreamt of.

Keep the spirit of the *Brickhouse Mindset* alive within you, and remember to Code Switch, Feed, Affirm & Believe in your dreams.

They are closer than you think!

Vibrate High My Dear Brickhouse!!

Thank you for allowing me to guide you on this transformative journey. Here's to the extraordinary life that awaits you!

Caio' for Now,

Che' Lovelight